DE.
DISSLCTED
IS THE DESIGN REAL?

Best wishes,

[signature]

DESIGN
DISSECTED
IS THE DESIGN REAL?

A CLINICAL LOOK AT LIFE'S COMPLEXITY, DESIGN AND ULTIMATE CAUSATION

DAVID J GALLOWAY

RITCHIE
John Ritchie Publishing
40 Beansburn, Kilmarnock, Scotland

ISBN-13: 978 1 914273 00 1

Copyright © 2021 David J Galloway

Copyright © 2021 by John Ritchie Ltd.
40 Beansburn, Kilmarnock, Scotland

www.ritchiechristianmedia.co.uk

Typeset by John Ritchie Ltd., Kilmarnock
Printed by Bell & Bain Ltd., Glasgow

Dedication

For Jack, and in memory of Eleanor, my parents: who, between them instilled in me the importance of diligence, taking responsibility, studying, and seeking truth wherever it may be found.

For Christine, my wife: for her love and support. She does try to sort out the wrinkles in my character and performance. I am in no position to assess how successful she has been but I do get the impression that it is an on-going project!

For Lynda and Jenni: our two daughters of whom I am rightly proud. What beautiful characters they have become.

Acknowledgements

I am indebted to many people (too many to mention) on whose knowledge and insight I have drawn to formulate my thinking with respect to the biggest questions of human existence – 'Where have we come from?' and 'What are we here for?' So many have unwittingly modelled and communicated clear analytical thinking which in turn has encouraged me to constructively examine the proffered, popular answers to these questions. Time and again these answers have failed to emerge from the evidence upon which they are supposed to rest. I am grateful that I can risk running the gauntlet of what appears to be accepted scientific wisdom and engage in that worthy discipline of questioning and testing the validity of the current consensus. This is an echo of the way scientific endeavour has advanced over hundreds of years.

I am grateful to those who encouraged me to embark on writing this book, including many colleagues, friends and members of the public who heard some of these ideas expressed in my valedictory lecture at the Royal College of Physicians and Surgeons of Glasgow in November 2018.

I acknowledge the help of those including Alastair Noble, David Williams, John West, and Evelyn Dunsmore who read and commented on early versions of the manuscript. I am grateful for those who have prepared messages of endorsement: John Lennox, Steve Meyer, Mike Behe, Doug Axe, Andy Bannister, David Williams and Frank Dunn. I am also very grateful for the interest and support from the staff of John Ritchie Ltd and I would particularly like to thank Alison Banks for her enthusiasm and guidance and Fraser Munro for his editing advice.

It has been a pleasure to work with Brian Chalmers of Brian Chalmers Design Services who has been the creative mind behind the internal design and layout. The cover was the result of a developing series of concepts and brought to completion by Julie Vatcher of Ripe Ideas Ltd.

I appreciate the many discussions and interactions with my friend and colleague Alastair Noble and I am honoured that he agreed to write the *Foreword*.

Finally to my wife, Christine, for her support. I sense that she (correctly) believes that many of the conclusions are self-evident, nevertheless she has tolerated the focused time and attention required to lay out the discussion and bring this project to the finishing line.

What others have said about 'Design Dissected'

For anyone who enjoys thinking about science and its implications, this book is a must read. Professor Galloway has spent his life in medical science. He packs his book with fascinating insights into the unbelievable complexity of human biochemistry and physiology. His prime interest is in demonstrating that there is real scientific evidence that the biosphere was designed for a purpose. He presents a series of telling challenges to naturalism and materialism, showing that they simply do not have the explanatory power to account for what science has revealed about the nature of life and consciousness. Throughout the book, personal anecdotes add much colour and interest to the journey on which he takes the reader. It is a journey well worth undertaking.

Professor John C Lennox MA MMath MA(Bioethics) DPhil PhD DSc
Emeritus Professor of Mathematics, University of Oxford Emeritus Fellow in
Mathematics and Philosophy of Science, Green Templeton College
Associate Fellow of the Said Business School
Author of *2084 Artificial Intelligence and the Future of Humanity*

In this beautifully written and extensively researched book, one of the United Kingdom's most distinguished medical scientists, David Galloway, brings a surgeon's skill to dissecting the complex and ultimate question of biological origins. He shows that a detailed examination of physiological systems in both the human body and the living cell reveals amazing information-rich molecules, hierarchies of modulation and engineering-style control systems. He argues that explaining the origin of such systematic organisation as a result of purely unguided natural processes stretches the limits of credulity. Instead, he makes a compelling case that this integrated and informational complexity provides powerful evidence of real, not just apparent, design. A fresh and original discussion of the evidence of intelligent design in living systems. Highly recommended!

Stephen C. Meyer PhD. *Cantab*
Director and Senior Fellow
Center for Science and Culture
Discovery Institute
Author of *Signature in the Cell: DNA and the Evidence of Intelligent Design*

By far the strongest evidence that a system was deliberately designed is the very structure of the system itself. When we discover multiple complex parts elegantly fitted to work with each other, the conclusion of purpose is irresistible. In *Design Dissected*, surgeon and academic, David Galloway, regales the reader with tale after tale of the wonders of the human body — and of the disasters that result when a part fails. By the end of the book, his conclusion that the body was purposely designed becomes self-evident.

Michael J. Behe PhD
Professor of Biochemistry
Lehigh University
Author of *Darwin's Black Box*

With surgical precision and entertaining book-side manner, David Galloway walks readers through all the subjects that contribute to a healthy understanding of the remarkable design of life. He brings history, philosophy, anatomy, medicine, and molecular biology together in a remarkably clear, concise, and convincing way. Highly recommended!

Douglas Axe PhD
Maxwell Professor of Molecular Biology
School of Science, Technology and Health
Biola University
Author of *Undeniable: How Biology Confirms Our Intuition That Life Was Designed*

Can science explain everything? In particular can it explain where life came from, why the universe is here, and why the deeper we look into nature the more evidence of design we see everywhere? In this wide ranging book, drawing on his many years of experience as a medic and a scientist, David Galloway helps the reader see that far from closing down discussion about ultimate questions, science opens them up. From the incredible complexity and intricate design in every one of our cells, to the carefully fine-tuned and interacting systems throughout the human body, to the fascinating questions raised by the human mind and consciousness, the reader is introduced to the wealth of evidence that design is the best explanation for what we see and experience all around us. Carefully researched, clearly presented, and illustrated with numerous fascinating stories from his many decades working in medicine around the world, this book is a blend of anecdote and philosophy, storytelling and science, to build a careful and convincing case that design is everywhere one looks. An important contribution to the discussion about whether materialism or theism is the best foundation, not just for questions about life and its purpose, but about the foundations of science itself. An engaging read.

Andy Bannister PhD
Director, Solas Centre for Public Christianity
Author of *The Atheist Who Didn't Exist*

To paraphrase a well-known legal judgment, it is for the evolutionist to prove the facts upon which they seek to rely. Such facts must be based on evidence and not just on suspicion or speculation. The evolutionist must set out the argument and demonstrate clearly why it is said the conclusion indeed follows from the facts. Or to paraphrase someone else, never let the evidence get in the way of a good argument.

In this book Professor Galloway puts the evidence, gained from his stellar career in medicine, front and centre, and lots of it - evidence the more fascinating and compelling because much of it exists within each one of us. And in doing so he presents an enormous, if not insurmountable, hurdle to the evolutionist. It turns out their conclusion does not follow from the facts, and the evidence more than gets in the way of their argument.

David Williams LLB (Hons) Lawyer
Author of *Taken Without Consent*

I had the privilege of attending the valedictory lecture delivered by Professor David Galloway as he stepped down from Presidency of The Royal College of Physicians and Surgeons of Glasgow. His title was an intriguing one, *Enigmata ad Infinitum*. I had no idea what we were about to hear but what emerged was one of the most memorable lectures I have attended in over 50 years in Medicine. David addressed the most complex questions relating to our planet and handled them in a logical and deeply knowledgeable way. In this, he drew on his considerable experience as a surgeon and clinician and interspersed this with his deep thinking on the origins of life, as we know it. I, and others, urged him to document this in a book and how well he has done this. Any concerns that this book is overpowering in its content and reasoning can be dispelled as David keeps the reader's interest alive, drawing on his deep knowledge of medicine, his impressive grasp of philosophy and his ability to see beyond the need for ultimate proof at a human level. I strongly recommend this most impressive and thought provoking book.

Professor Francis G Dunn CBE DL DSc MB ChB
FRCP(Glasg,Edin,Lond) FACC FACP(Hon) FRCPI(Hon)
Professor of Cardiovascular Science
University of Glasgow

CONTENTS

Foreword

It is an honour for me to write a foreword to this remarkable book by my friend and colleague, Prof David Galloway, who has a prodigious reputation as a skilled clinician and, as a past President of the Royal College of Physicians and Surgeons of Glasgow, an effective representative of the wider interests of the medical fraternity. He is now increasingly being recognised as a skilled communicator in Christian apologetics, combining medical and scientific insights in his approach.

In this book, David explores in some detail contemporary arguments in science and faith, now generally regarded as being in irresolvable conflict. This book should convince the reader that this is far from the case. David's extensive knowledge of medicine enables him to open a new front in the debate about design in nature. Some of the examples he draws from anatomy and physiology are breath-taking in their precision and sophistication. Although the content may at first sound challenging, the author combines historical and personal dimensions in a light and easily accessible style.

There are three main themes to the book. Firstly, the suffocating tyranny of 'the scientific consensus' is demonstrated in several historical examples where it became a clear obstacle to progress. Secondly, the existence of overlapping layers of complexity in biological systems is explored in some impressive examples taken from the author's clinical experience. Thirdly, the profound mystery of human consciousness is explored. The general conclusion David draws for current theories of origins is that a 'transcendent agency', however much it is blithely dismissed, provides a much more coherent scientific explanation for the complexity of nature than mere chance or necessity.

In our age, we are accustomed to definitive and elaborate expositions of 'the scientific consensus', in areas as diverse as climate change, COVID-19, or the origin of life. The scathing criticism that descends upon those who beg to disagree is all too obvious. In this book, David shows how blindly defending the 'consensus' is not how science and medicine advanced, but rather by the hard-won acceptance of radical ideas which were originally dismissed with derision. In this regard he describes several areas of medicine where the breakthroughs came from brave individuals who were willing to challenge the consensus with indisputable evidence for their case.

From an understanding of human anatomy and physiology, David identifies several examples of complexity and control within living systems that defy any explanation in terms of random chance. One, which I had never encountered before, is the way in which the blood flow at the moment of birth switches almost instantly from the mother's placenta to the infant's lungs. Any slip up here, and the infant is gone; raising the legitimate question as to how such a system could possibly evolve, through the accumulation of many small random changes, with such exquisite and crucial precision.

In the third section of his book, David explores the truly mysterious world of consciousness, the loss of which he is thoroughly familiar with, having frequently used anaesthetics in surgery. However, that is trivial in comparison with the real but immaterial phenomenon of our minds and brains. David's treatment of this area shows convincingly that a chance or evolutionary explanation of consciousness is untenable.

This is a remarkable book, which argues cogently, from some less well-known examples, the overwhelming case for design in nature. It is a book to read, enjoy, study, and discuss. Perhaps in the debate around origins we should listen as much to doctors and clinicians as to biologists and chemists!

Alastair Noble PhD
Former Schools' Inspector for Science and
Assistant Director of Education
Glasgow, Scotland. September 2020

Introduction

The mystery of how living things came to be and to take the form that they do has been the focus of much investigation and debate for centuries. Many people assert that all of reality, including life, has simply emerged as a result of natural law and circumstance. How credible is that assumption? How well does it fit with what we find? Exquisite features of apparent design are in evidence everywhere we look. Getting down to basics, we can say with confidence that either *something* is responsible for all the molecular engineering of life or, it just happened and *nothing* is directly responsible. Which option offers the best explanation?

The theme of this book concerns the evidence for design in the complexity of life and it assembles an argument to challenge the conventional assumption that the source of the amazing systems in living things is entirely natural.

My purpose is to provide a clinician's perspective on the evidence for real design in living things. While it is written at a popular level, there are some technical details but these will be accessible to everyone. Those with a basic understanding of human biology or a background in healthcare will immediately connect with many of the examples. I have chosen some actual clinical cases to illustrate particular points or to provide a backdrop to the argument as it develops. I have also tried to explore some of the amazing connected systems that exist in immunology, endocrinology, physiology, biochemistry and neuroscience. Specific design scenarios are described, such as the astonishing changes that have to take place in the human circulatory system when the placental oxygen delivery is switched off and the lungs suddenly have to come into operation at the time of birth. Had that system failed to operate for you – you would not be reading this sentence!

The structure of the book is built around three sections. Firstly, in **Enigmata**, I have outlined the means by which the great questions of science have been tackled. We will see how scientific truth has sometimes even been ridiculed before finding acceptance. We'll discover how scientific conclusions can be contaminated by presuppositions of various kinds and consider reductionism as an enterprise to uncovering causation. To put it another way we need to address the question of whether we can support the idea that natural processes are entirely sufficient to produce what we find in the living world, or not? I also offer a warning about the dangers of scientism – that is, the assumption that science is equipped to answer every ultimate question.

The second section, **Layers of Perplexity**, aims to reveal why the conventional understanding about the origin of life and of biological complexity fails to carry the intellectual weight it is required to bear. I have used examples from human systems and even considered the discipline of origin of life chemistry. Each of these demonstrates that a naturalistic understanding offers a completely inadequate explanation for the intricate and nuanced systems that underpin our existence.

The final section, **Thinking about Thinking**, opens the mystery of the origin of consciousness and asks the questions of ultimate reality that, for many, seem to be just too difficult and are therefore consigned to the 'consider it later' pile!

The conclusion may not be palatable for some but the evidence included in this book exposes the reality that neither the origin of life, nor complex biological systems nor even consciousness can be explained by a natural mechanism and that a transcendent agency has better explanatory power. This book provides a powerful challenge to the naturalistic or materialistic view that the universe and life results from unguided 'natural' processes and numerous strands of evidence accumulate to show just how untenable such a view really is. The case for real, rather than illusory, design is powerful and persuasive. It is time to consign outdated thinking and theories to the scrap heap rather than trying to resuscitate ideas that fly in the face of the evidence.

Section 1
Enigmata

Death in Vienna and the birth of an idea

First they ignore you, then they ridicule you, then they fight you, then you win.

Mahatma Gandhi [1869-1948]

IT WAS SIMPLY SCANDALOUS. Tragedy followed upon tragedy. Hospitals ought to be safe places. We know, of course, that even today they are not as safe as they could or should be, but back in 19th century Vienna patients were dying for no very obvious reason. It was desperate! With the view afforded by hindsight we can see quite clearly what the problem really was. But at the time, the answers were certainly not in plain sight. They were, however, not far away and with some careful scientific detective work, painstaking enquiry, sound reasoning, and a little time, it all became clear.

The famous and historic city of Vienna had seen more than its fair share of turmoil. Napoleon conquered it twice in the early part of the century. However it soon became an influential centre of political power as well as being recognised for its impressive architecture and industry.

In the 1830s all was not well in the notorious General Hospital. An unacceptably large proportion of young mothers died of overwhelming infection and it was such a public concern that many prayed they would not be admitted there to give birth. There was what could only be described as an outbreak of puerperal (also known as childbed) fever that carried a typical mortality rate of 10%-15%. The peak death rate came in October 1842 and reached almost 30% - no wonder there was such alarm in the community. Not only that, while it might be expected that standards would improve and childbirth would become safer, the death rate was dramatically worse than that revealed in the records from 30 years before. The maternity unit had two sections, Ward 1 being the area with the shocking reputation. In Ward 2, the death rate was steady at around 3%, a figure that was considered acceptable in hospitals at that time.

Ignaz Semmelweis [1818-1865] was a Hungarian doctor who was appointed to the role of assistant physician in the Vienna General Hospital in 1846. His particular responsibility concerned the care of women in childbirth and he was curious about the contrasting results in the two maternity sections. Semmelweis took a logical look at the data and found that the risk of maternal death for the entire hospital shot up in the year 1823 – this was the same year that some of the medical student teaching in pathology involved attendance at post mortem examinations. What he observed was alarming in the extreme. The policies in the two wards were similar, the only real difference being that the births were supervised by the qualified doctors assisted by medical students in Ward 1 and by the midwifery pupils in Ward 2. During his time there, Semmelweis observed the effect of having these staff groups change places. It was quickly obvious that the high mortality rate then applied to Ward 2! They decided on a very modern policy – they closed the section for a while, only to find on its re-opening, and with the medical students still at work, the results were as bad as ever.

As is often the case in a conundrum such as this, there was a key moment when a route to clarifying an important element of the puzzle presented itself. Unfortunately for Semmelweis, it involved the death of a close colleague in the early part of March 1847. When news broke about what had happened to Professor Jakob

Kolletschka, he was 'overwhelmed by the sad news.'[1] Kolletschka was the academic lead for Forensic Medicine and frequently performed post mortem examinations. In the course of one of these autopsies his finger was pricked with a contaminated knife held by one of his students. Initially, and over a few days, he developed some swelling and redness, at first arising in his hand and progressively moving up his arm. Before long, he developed full-blown sepsis syndrome (the terminology used to describe the response mounted by the body to an invasive infection. The effects can be widespread and far-reaching, involving significant threat to the function of every organ system). For poor Kolletschka, he even developed a septic focus or abscess in one eye. This was when the light of understanding came on for Semmelweis. He later wrote, 'I could see clearly that the disease from which Kolletschka died was identical to that from which so many hundred maternity patients had also died. The maternity patients also had lymphangitis, peritonitis, pericarditis, pleurisy, and meningitis, and metastases also formed in many of them. Day and night I was haunted by the image of Kolletschka's disease and was forced to recognise, ever more decisively, that the disease from which Kolletschka died was identical to that from which so many maternity patients died.'[1]

So, with a combination of data, rational analysis, and creative thinking, Semmelweis understood what distinguished the two wards. It was the fact that medical students would frequently come straight from the post mortem room and examine patients in labour without any thought of hand hygiene. His view was that it was related to particles of tissue from the deceased patients somehow gaining access to the circulation of the maternity cases and resulting in puerperal fever and death for so many. Hand washing was not a regular feature of clinical practice in Vienna, or indeed anywhere else in the 19th century, so Semmelweis insisted that, following exposure to any post mortem examination, the staff wash their hands thoroughly in chlorinated water. The effect on death rates in young mothers was dramatic - the incidence fell to around a tenth of the previous level.

The ideas advanced by Semmelweis, like many brilliant insights in medical practice, met with influential opposition. You would think that the observable facts would speak for themselves, but you would be wrong. Several prominent physicians, including the famous obstetrician in Edinburgh, James Young Simpson, whose claim to fame was the introduction of chloroform for its anaesthetic properties, was rather unmoved by the work from Vienna. We are left to wonder how many more lives were needlessly lost because clinicians either did not bother about the questions of causation of puerperal sepsis, were disinclined to follow the evidence, or for some other vindictive reason made no effort to adopt the changes which would have made such a difference to outcome. There was a cry for a mechanism to link the hand hygiene with whatever might be transmitted to the patients, thus putting them in serious danger. No satisfactory mechanism was known at that stage – Pasteur, the famous microbiologist in Paris, and Lister, the Professor of Surgery in Glasgow, both of whom made huge contributions to the understanding of surgical infection, did not make the necessary connections for at least another quarter of a century. Because of the furore linked to his unpopularity, the hapless Semmelweis was vilified and at the end of his contract at the hospital in 1849, it was not renewed – despite the fact that the mortality rates had by this time reached a new low. He was widely opposed, even by the famous Rudolf Virchow, now regarded as the father of modern pathology and with hindsight, it almost looks as though there was a trend, around Europe, to reject the teaching of Semmelweis – even although it was not only correct but was the most beneficial and influential development of its time. Not only did he become obsessed with the issue, he was not noted for a gentle tactful approach towards colleagues with whom he disagreed and the whole episode drove him to drink and to become increasingly antagonistic towards his opponents. He wrote open letters to other obstetricians expressing his vicious anger and accusing them of murderous indifference. He became more and more mentally unstable and he was finally and

24

tragically tricked into being admitted to a mental institution. By the time he recognised the deception, he was unable to escape, was badly beaten by the guards, bound in a straitjacket and consigned to solitary confinement in an unlit cell. During the altercation, it is likely that he sustained a wound to his right hand and ironically this became infected and he died within a couple of weeks at the age of 47 on August 13th 1865. The post mortem confirmed the cause of his death to be 'pyaemia' another term for what we sometimes call blood poisoning – systemic infection!

The so-called Semmelweis effect is a description of an almost determined rejection of new knowledge, perhaps because of the challenge it makes to accepted dogma. The result is that outdated, incorrect, and entrenched beliefs or paradigms survive the revelation of accurate new information.

An additional irony is that the very day before Semmelweis died an 11-year-old trauma patient called James Greenlees was admitted to the Royal Infirmary in Glasgow under the care of the then relatively new Professor of Surgery, Joseph Lister. James has been run over by a cart and sustained a compound fracture of his left tibia and fibula. This was no minor injury. A fracture is described as 'compound' when the bone fragments penetrate the skin. The risk of infection with whatever organisms were present in the muck from the road or even from the patient's clothes or skin was very high. In those days, such an injury carried about a 90% chance of the need for subsequent amputation because of gangrene and around a 50:50 chance of death. So for young James, not only was there a major question mark over his possible survival but there was a significant chance that this would prove to be a life changing injury. Lister, however, was developing a new approach to address the risk of the surgical sepsis that carried such a high mortality. James was the first and most dramatic success story in the practical assault on infection, based on what was known at the time as the germ theory of putrefaction. Even Lister, who was also proved to be correct in his understanding, ran into a sceptical reception. I recall looking with dismay at the response of his contemporaries, as recorded in the account made of the meeting at which he presented his theory in the Faculty of Physicians and Surgeons of Glasgow on April 17th 1868.[2] The minutes of the meeting include this excerpt – "Mr Lister gave a lengthened exposition of the atmospheric germ theory of putrefaction, and illustrated it by the exhibition of M. Pasteur's experiment" referring here to a demonstration Louis Pasteur had made in Paris. It goes on, "He next directed attention to the employment of carbolic acid for the destruction of the germs *presumed* to exist in the air, and which Mr Lister *supposed* to be the exciting cause of putrefaction in wounds." The gory details of a young man who had sustained a stab wound to his chest then follows and the transcript of the account is held by the Royal College of Physicians and Surgeons of Glasgow. To say that the attitude of the minute secretary was somewhat sceptical would be an understatement! It was, in some ways, reminiscent of the Semmelweis experience.

After some considerable time, the accumulating observational evidence began to gain wide acceptance. The work of Pasteur in France and Lister in Glasgow began to piece together a coherent mechanism that adequately accounted for the observations Semmelweis made in Vienna twenty years before.

It is such a shame that, even now, the truth is sometimes not only not accepted, it is commonly rejected and even ridiculed. It makes one thoughtful about taking on established scientific dogma. However, that is what a scientific mind-set needs to accomplish. That is exactly why scientific enquiry has been so incredibly successful and influential in shaping our modern world. While we shy away from cogent interpretations of observed reality at our peril, there is no shortage of scientists who are so totally wedded to finding natural explanations for life's complexity that they are willing to sacrifice common sense in order to avoid the conclusion that real design provides the best fit.

It may not be possible to establish a tight set of proofs, but a system of understanding that could provide some satisfactory answers to the big questions of life would provide at least some clarity, where currently we stumble around in an intellectual fog. We could all use some answers, especially when we come to consider the most perplexing questions about, for example, what life really is; what are the basic differences between the animate and the inanimate? Is it possible that within their characteristics, living things betray some key features which help us reach satisfactory answers, and maybe even shed some light on what purpose there may be? There remain, of course, those ultimate questions about the cosmos and about life – where did it all come from and how did it get going? Everyone grapples with these issues at some stage. Many conclude that no answers are available and give up. I would suggest that a negative approach like that is bound to be unproductive and would like, from a consideration of our current knowledge, experience, and reasoning, to suggest that we can derive some very confident conclusions for some of these questions. For sure, there is no shortage of proffered answers; indeed, we hear a cacophony of different voices seeking to offer their insights. Some of the most respected scientific academics of our day have made thought-provoking contributions to this puzzling area and we really ought to take care to evaluate the answers that have been proposed.

I have no doubt that we can discover a great deal by addressing some of these difficult questions. We may not be in a position to solve all the puzzles, but there is no doubt that we can advance our understanding about the nature and origin of our world by an approach involving the same ingredients used by Semmelweis, Lister, and Pasteur. By absorbing the data, employing analysis and reason, we can make significant inroads into conundrums that have perplexed people for centuries.

Furthermore, there is much we can discover about the nature and origin of human life and by implication we can infer real insights into the question of the purpose of life. These are some of the

27

perplexing issues that seem to have evaded satisfactory explanation, at least thus far. How did all this happen? Was it simply a series of happy accidents or is there some intentionality behind the world in which we live? Is there sufficient evidence to infer that all the complexity, diversity, and apparent intentionality of life is meant to be the way it is or is it just the way the cookie crumbled? We need to weigh up the case that some make for an accidental, purposeless universe. It remains a burning question - is the evident design real or just an illusion?

So, where can we look for some answers? I have found it interesting and entertaining to plough around in my own field of interest. My training is in clinical medicine and surgery and I have had the amazing privilege of working as a surgeon, treating patients with all manner of problems ranging from trauma (why is it that people are still inclined to stick sharp things into each other?) to cancer in all its forms. Along the way, I have had to learn to deal with a large range of other conditions and I think it might be interesting to start in that world because there are certainly questions to ask, clues to uncover and fascinating insights to pick up. Inevitably, as we explore the controversy about the role of design, some of these clinical topics will provoke subsequent questions; indeed layer upon layer of questions, leading us progressively to more fundamental areas. Working our way into this hierarchy of mystery, we will consider how these characteristics and systems came to be. Understanding causation and dissecting that out provides remarkable insight and understanding into how the machinery of life works. So many of these biological systems are exquisite, complex, balanced, and super efficient – by what mechanism could they possibly arise? Are we even close to understanding this? They seem to bear some of the characteristics of designed systems; they have purposefully arranged components, staggering intricacy, and highly efficient functional parts. Did this all just happen by the action of natural law and happenstance? It is certainly a common view that the natural world came to its present state by purely physical and chemical processes, with the filtering help of natural selection. There are, as we shall see, aspects of this view that defy common sense. While that doesn't necessarily mean to say that our common sense is unreliable, it does mean that it is surely worth questioning the truth of the matter. Could it be that the apparent design in the cosmos is real?

Take home message ...

The scientific endeavour has been extraordinarily successful in unravelling the mysteries of life. Despite that, it remains somewhat tarnished as a means to search for truth. All too often, the plain and obvious conclusions are avoided in preference to a favoured theory or idea. The history of such contamination of genuine scientific enquiry can result in the persistence of a fashionable idea that, in reality, gets in the way of the truth.

The conundrum rumbles on - seismic puzzles

A tornado of thought is unleashed after each new insight. This in turn results in an earthquake of assumptions.

Vera Nazarian [1966-]

JUST AFTER 9:30AM ON NOVEMBER 11th 2018, there was a low grade earthquake-like perturbation which triggered sensors as far as 11,000 miles apart – from near Madagascar off the east coast of Africa to South America, and even as far away as New Zealand and Hawaii.[3] Seismologists have developed a pretty good understanding of the way in which tension builds up in tectonic plates that make up the surface of the crust of the Earth. When this suddenly releases, there is often a massive burst of energy, apparent in the form of an earthquake or even a tsunami. Commonly the initial so-called primary fast compression waves are the most vigorous and then slightly lower energy secondary waves follow – these also tend to have a relatively high frequency. The detectors which picked up the rumbling activity close to the coast of the island of Mayotte recorded low grade, low frequency waves and it is not at all clear where they came from or why they reached around the globe as far as they did. Perhaps there was indeed a build-up of tension and a kind of slow earthquake that triggered these as the pressure was gradually released.

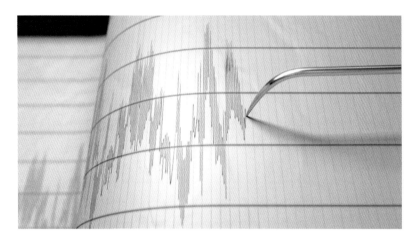

Alternatively, some think that there may be a big lake of molten rock or magma under the sea that is changing configuration and position and causing the disturbance. Whatever the explanation, there are teams of seismologists working to establish a clearer sense of what the cause may be. This is the way the scientific approach to dissecting causation works. Irrespective of the discipline, it gathers the evidence and applies methodical reasoning and, sometimes, observation and experimentation to reach a conclusion.

To my mind, we routinely need a clinical, logical, and scientific approach to probe which explanation provides the best fit for any data. It is helpful to apply an accepted scientific approach to make sense of what can be observed. Understanding how things come to be is an important step to figuring out exactly how they work.

In the clinical world, the process usually encompasses several steps and you will see how these are used in real examples in this book. First, it is important to try to define clearly the situation that requires to be explained. Then we need to focus on accumulating relevant data in order to draw up a list of possible explanations. These can then be whittled down progressively by excluding those causes that fail to provide a good fit for the data, thus narrowing down the options to identify the particular cause that satisfies most or all of the necessary criteria.

As we discovered, hospitals can be dangerous places. When the actual statistics relating to adverse events of various kinds affecting hospitalised patients were published, many clinicians could hardly believe what they were seeing. For surgical patients, the lack of a safety culture in some healthcare systems became headline news in the wake of surgical disasters that, with appropriate care, would have been prevented. Stories abound of wrong side or wrong site surgery. You would hardly credit that operations have even been done on the wrong patient! In any human endeavour there is always the possibility of error of judgment, but some of the totally preventable errors that are worryingly common in healthcare include the classical errors of omission, where steps in a process are missed out. Sometimes harm results when procedures are followed incorrectly or are sequenced badly. Even timing errors can be troublesome, with things being done correctly, but too slowly, too quickly or too late. This is such a large problem that, in the USA, if deaths resulting from healthcare were considered a disease, it would be the third most significant killer behind cardiovascular disease and cancer in its various forms.[4]

The frequency of adverse events in UK hospitals is similar, with around 10% of patients experiencing some kind of harm. Around 50% of these are considered completely preventable and about a third of these errors or problems result in harm or even death. When you try to understand the perspective by comparing with other activities that carry measurable risk, much less than 1 death is likely to occur in every 100,000 encounters for those working in the nuclear power industry, travelling on European railroads or on scheduled airlines. More risky activities like driving a car or working in the chemical manufacturing industry carry an estimated fatality risk of somewhere between one per 1,000 and one per 100,000 encounters. The really risky activities where a risk of greater than 1 death per 1,000 encounters applies, include bungee jumping, extreme mountaineering and, perhaps surprisingly, being a patient in a modern hospital. Disturbing as that may be, it has at least concentrated much effort to try to understand what the causes might be and to address these, with a view to encouraging a proper safety culture. A great deal of progress has been made in understanding the various and complex factors which cohere and thus put patients at risk. It is no easy task to sort out the relative causes within complex organisations delivering diverse, customised, and complex packages of care. Thinking about individual decisions and the strategy used to make them, is as important as a consideration of how the whole system of care works. For each scenario the key objectives must be to identify the particular problem and, crucially, pin down the respective cause.

The importance of aetiology, the study of the causes of disease, and indeed the principles of dissecting out relevant causes apply across a range of disciplines. As far as earthquakes are concerned, there is general agreement that the underlying cause is the release of the tension that can build up where two or more tectonic plates come into contact. As they move one against the other, the pressure builds and ultimately something has to give. The effects can be varied and include violent shaking or liquefaction of the earth's surface or perhaps the production of a tidal wave. While there may be a cogent appreciation of the general causes and even an identification of the fault lines at risk, it has always proved difficult to translate that understanding into any kind of confident or accurate prediction as to what might happen and when. Many questions remain.

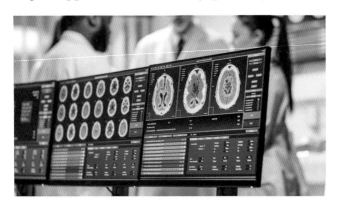

Much the same tends to apply to cause detection in medical and surgical care and it is often possible to come close to the truth, even although additional questions are generated along the way. When a patient presents with abdominal pain, we need to entertain a host of possibilities – could it be some inflammatory problem like appendicitis or is there a blockage somewhere? – perhaps a kidney stone or a gallstone or might it be some much less common condition? As we shall discover, cause detection can get us close to the truth in the more fundamental life sciences like physiology and biochemistry. These topics are so basic to figuring out the cause of abnormal function and disease. The unravelling of the various parts of a biological system can provide exactly the information required to make adjustments, fix faults and even gain control of a particular system or process. This, for example, has been the basis for developing certain drugs that specifically block particular metabolic pathways or immune functions, or even in providing the tools to control aspects of how and whether cells may divide and reproduce. Some of the physiological and biochemical systems are not only mind-bogglingly complex and gloriously detailed, but we can actually draw some very confident conclusions about their origin. When we begin to dig into how some of these amazing systems came to be, we'll sometimes generate as many questions as answers, but this is exactly how scientific understanding advances.

As we encounter some selected examples amongst the completely perplexing riddle of life we will need to grapple with causation along the way, even drilling down to questions concerning how the chemistry of life itself arose. Just as the seismic waves from near Madagascar appeared mysteriously and spread around the planet, so the enigma of the origin of life and even the origin of the universe itself rumbles on. So too, the complex causation responsible for systemic failures in health care delivery makes for as many questions as answers. There are other perplexing topics too, but let's start and see what kind of sense we can make of the biosphere in which we live. We'll get to the weird and wonderful later, when we dabble with quantum reality and the source of consciousness! For now, let me bring you into my world – the weird and wonderful clinical world of people and their problems.

Take home message ...

To fully understand any phenomenon there is a fundamental need to understand its cause. Therein lies the key to unravelling both mechanisms and implications.

Surgeons are sane – I'm not so sure about the others!

Sometimes wrong but never in doubt.

Anon

I N CLINICAL PRACTICE, AS IN other disciplines, attempting to gain an understanding of the cause or aetiology of some condition can reveal much about its nature. When I was a medical student, it was with some trepidation that I embarked on an attachment in psychiatry. The whole discipline seemed a bit strange. I saw myself as a budding surgeon – I was keen to get on with sorting and straightening, removing, unblocking, and redirecting. That's what surgeons do and to be honest while we have developed an impressive and sometimes impenetrable language all of our own, the basics are not too difficult. Basically it is down to re-shaping, re-wiring, re-plumbing, and quite often re-moving! Psychiatry, on the other hand, is a totally different ball game! Weird and wonderful, surprising and unpredictable. I can think of a couple of patients who, although they were not aware of it, taught me some vital lessons that have real relevance and application beyond the world of healthcare. Let me tell you about two incidents and you will soon see how both of these lessons apply to the way we think about the wider problems which are encountered in trying to make sense of the world.

As a young doctor, one of the most important skills to master is to develop the ability to uncover and properly understand what a patient has been experiencing. It is a matter of unravelling the history of their symptoms and, by examination, detecting any relevant physical signs. I learned early on, when I had the opportunity to practice my history-taking skills with patients who were the worse for wear after an evening in the hostelries of Glasgow, that trying to take a coherent account of what the patient may feel to be wrong could be quite a challenge. When someone has been over-indulging in what we might euphemistically call hydroxylated hydrocarbons, 'alcohol' to you and me, often the resulting conversations with such individuals were both bizarre and irrational. Sometimes they could even be threatening, and when an individual begins to demonstrate the effects of alcohol withdrawal, some really bizarre things can take place.

I well remember going into the consulting room where a middle-aged man was cowering and obviously terrified. He had recoiled into a corner of the room, sweating and shaking, scared stiff of the horrific creatures that he thought were threatening him. These were hallucinations of course, but try telling him that! Now, quite why this happens is not really understood. We have a much clearer understanding as a result of attempting to dissect out the cause, but whether and how much some neuro-transmitter chemicals are down-regulated whilst others are up-regulated and quite why some parts of the central nervous system are more likely to be involved in the process than others remains in the realm of speculation and hypothesis. All of this served to illustrate just how mysterious brain function can be. At least in these circumstances we know enough to say that, even although the exact mechanisms resulting in the features of delirium tremens are not yet understood, there is one thing we do understand. It can be very quickly reversed (albeit temporarily), by giving a small dose of the very drug that is responsible. A solution, which medical practitioners are agreed, is not the best! There are alternatives that can smooth the road to recovery without the risk of compounding the problem further. It is far better to offer definitive treatment and try to correct the problem, rather than just make the symptoms go away.

In fact, taking refuge as I did, away from the occasional madness of the Emergency Department with its attendant Friday night delirium and confusion, I repaired instead to the surgical wards. But I was caught out even here, and was given a brilliant illustration of how even surgeons can sometimes get to grips with and disentangle causation when the brain appears to misbehave.

Portrait of Karl Friedrich Hieronymus von Münchausen (19th century) by G. Bruckner, Museum of Münchausen in Bodenwerder, Germany.

I was also introduced to the amazing tale of Karl Friedrich Hieronymus von Münchausen, who had been born into an aristocratic family in lower Saxony in May 1720. While he was something of a celebrity in his lifetime, he became a medical celebrity some 231 years later! Before I tell you my patient's story, let me explain. In the late 1730s, von Münchausen served in a Russian cavalry regiment and saw action in some skirmishes with the Turkish military in 1740 and 1741. He retired from the army with the rank of Captain at the age of 40.

His lifestyle was apparently seasoned by many parties that were often frequented by the social elite and von Münchausen developed the reputation as an entertaining raconteur. Not only was he a gifted storyteller, he was, it seems, frequently inclined to exaggerate and embellish his military exploits and he gained considerable notoriety to the point that his parties became very popular as his reputation spread. Interestingly, the real von Münchausen became the model for a fictional character known as Baron Münchausen, whose defining characteristics were becoming embroiled in ridiculous and sometimes comical adventures where the most improbable and illogical solutions were used to rescue him from some pitfall or extract him from some danger.

In 1951, a paper written by a well-known and particularly insightful physician called Richard Asher was published in the *British Medical Journal*.[5] Asher was an astute clinical thinker and made some very important contributions in his day. One of them was to describe what has become known as Münchausen's syndrome. This almost certainly resulted from his ability to categorise certain patients he encountered as he supervised what was the mental observation ward in the Central Middlesex Hospital in London. As he observed the patients under his care, he realised that some patients not only attended frequently with a suite of unexplained symptoms, but that many of them were making a habit of going from hospital to hospital with the same story and each time the explanation for their problem remained a mystery. There were some common features however. They were more likely to be young men and, like the cases I saw, they tended to complain of severe abdominal pain. They would typically writhe in discomfort, display cleverly manipulative behaviour, demand opiate drugs, and so exaggerate their 'illness' that they would even manage to hoodwink surgical teams to carry out emergency surgery for a presumed intra-abdominal catastrophe. They frequently ended up with many surgical scars as they moved from hospital to hospital and area to area, pulling off the same confidence trick again and again. The operations always turned out to be negative – they revealed no significant abnormality. When their cover was blown – sometimes by a clinician who had encountered them in another hospital and remembered the scenario, or as a result of consistently negative test results or fruitless surgery - these patients would often exhibit defensive and even aggressive behaviour towards the staff, only to head off somewhere else and again demonstrate this pathological need to have treatment with heavy duty pain killers or surgery. Asher cleverly recognised and classified several different collections of features and labelled the cases accordingly, although the range and diversity of the way they attempt to engineer treatment is almost limitless. The essential components that were required to make the diagnosis included the simulated illness accompanied by pathological lying and the tendency to wander from place to place and hospital to hospital.

So, back to my patient who was an intelligent and very plausible young woman. She had endured several hospital admissions over many months and the clinical teams had always failed to make a confident diagnosis. She had a secure professional role in a dental surgery, was apparently happily married and seemingly bemused and really worried about the way she regularly lost consciousness, developed profound weakness with the inability to move her limbs and usually ended up being admitted to hospital as an emergency. I had seen her several times in repeated admissions over a period of two or three months and as we had investigated her carefully and thoroughly, we began to consider the possibility that she might have Münchausen's syndrome. I confess that, in this particular case, I really found that diagnosis pretty difficult to believe until it was revealed in graphic and dramatic style. The consultant surgeon in charge of our team was making morning rounds and we moved from bed to bed, visiting the patients who had been admitted over the previous night. The rounds were interrupted by a commotion because, having been admitted again overnight, this particular girl collapsed and was found lying on the floor, completely unresponsive. The team gathered round to assess the situation and provide whatever help we could. She was unconscious, breathing normally, her vital signs were normal but she was completely flaccid

41

and not making any response to pain. Occasional flickering of the eyelids was, in retrospect, a tell-tale sign, although quite how it might all fit together remained a mystery. Even when people have significant impairment of conscious level, it is usual for a standard painful stimulus to elicit some characteristic movement. It may be localisation and withdrawal from the source of the pain, but even when people have a serious brain injury and are genuinely deeply unconscious they will commonly demonstrate limb flexion or extension in response to a standard painful stimulus. Remarkably, in this case, there was nothing. Not a flicker. Bizarre. Then the boss hit on an idea and as there were several junior clinicians and medical students present, and with the bed screens drawn, he made as if to convert this situation into a teaching scenario. He described how while it was unusual, some patients would actually feign unconsciousness. Clearly this was exactly what he suspected here. He also explained that there was a sure-fire way to determine if someone was genuinely unconscious and it related to the way the nervous system produced muscle tone in patients who were genuinely unconscious as opposed to those who may be malingerers. He continued: "if someone is really unconscious, you can lift one of their limbs into a particular position and the involuntary muscle tone will hold that position. If the patient is feigning unconsciousness, however, the limb will collapse, completely flaccid, on the bed." Of course, the picture he painted was complete nonsense but was simply designed to see if the patient could be deceived into demonstrating the true nature of the malady. Well, to my astonishment, he lifted her arm off the bed to almost ninety degrees from the horizontal and, after a moment, let it go. There she lay, apparently deeply unconscious and unrousable, with her arm in the air! Diagnosis made – this was a case of a self-induced factitious disorder - Münchausen's syndrome! We never really did understand why she presented the way she did, but at least it allowed a proper understanding that her neuromuscular symptoms and signs did not betray any serious underlying neurological disease. I have encountered many patients with such factitious conditions and it is annoying that they waste resources to their own ultimate harm. It is little wonder that Richard Asher, writing a letter to the *British Medical Journal* in December 1958 in response to a report of six cases, closed out his letter with a wonderful phrase, reminiscent of a Churchillian wartime quotation, "Never in the history of hospitals have so many doctors been so much annoyed by so few patients."[6]

Whatever the cause of the variants of Münchausen's syndrome and there are many, many examples, it is amazing the lengths to which some people will go in order to convince themselves and others that the correct conclusion differs from what the evidence suggests.

I suggest to you that these two cases illustrate important principles that need to be kept in mind as we grapple with some of the issues we will encounter in considering the possible role of design in nature. First, treating delirium tremens with alcohol would be wonderfully effective in the short term but does not get to the root of the problem. Sometimes we need to challenge and probe rather deeper than taking the easy option and adopting the simplest possible explanation. Secondly, when someone settles on a particular set of beliefs, they will sometimes go to extraordinary lengths to make the theory fit the data! This happens in the science world as well as the medical world. Maybe this is an important reason for the 'Semmelweis effect' that we encountered earlier. Indeed, there is even some evidence to suggest that the greater the level of education a person has, the more inclined they are to do all sorts of intellectual somersaults to try to maintain a belief system, even when the evidence points in a different direction. We will see how these traps catch out the unwary scientific thinkers in the next few chapters.

Take home message ...

The correct explanation may not be the easiest or most appealing explanation. Simply accepting a consensus can avoid resistance. Challenging a consensus can be tough, but, as history has shown, it can also lead one closer to the truth.

Transcendent turtles and questions - all the way down

So, what do we do when we encounter a big problem? Well, depending on the circumstances we might panic, although that is unlikely to provide a constructive solution. Typically, to take a cold hard look at a difficult or a puzzling situation we need a cool head and a logical approach.

When I was a youngster I lived near an ancient and iconic large volcanic basalt plug located on the north bank of the River Clyde in the West of Scotland, close to the centre of Dumbarton. Dumbarton

Dumbarton Castle from the south bank of the River Clyde.

45

Rock has been the location of the oldest defensive stronghold in Scotland and there are historical records reaching as far back as the 5th century.

The ancient Britons, the Picts, and the Romans all feature in its long history. It was even traded by the Earl of Lennox when he tried to bargain some English land as well as setting up a marriage pact with Henry VIII for the hand of his niece. Later in that decade Mary, Queen of Scots was imprisoned there, being held for several months as she awaited embarkation for France and safety in the summer of 1548. Apart from its romantic past it was a great place for rock climbing adventures! Depending on which section of the rock we determined to climb, as boys we sometimes found ourselves in precarious and sometimes very scary situations – often complicated by the incoming tide and the risk of being well and truly stranded! I was never a confident climber and can well remember following more agile and confident friends as they scaled up the steep rock face only to look down and instantly realise that I was in some considerable difficulty. Somehow, getting up seemed easier than coming down and the true enormity of the risk of descent became more apparent upon looking down at the boulders and the tidal river far below. So, how to solve the problem? Panicking was never productive although I regularly felt the rising anxiety as I considered my predicament on these occasions. On reflection, taking my time to plan a careful, if not risk-free route, and doing it in small manageable stages proved to be the best solution. Having gained some downward progress, a repeat of the policy of thinking about the least nerve-wracking route and slowly picking my way down, allowed survival and avoided the embarrassing outcome of having to voice my inner feelings and appear to be less capable than my peers. Looking back, risking life and limb to save face doesn't really seem like such a good idea.

Big problems can often be broken down into smaller components. Asking and answering the questions that emerge from the smaller problems can generate some real insight into the big problem and at the very least we can hope to edge our way towards a solution. So that is the approach we will take here. We'll start in a fairly classical and time-honoured fashion. I always find it more satisfying to try to make sense of the world around me, but to do so in ways that lead to some understanding. It is far better to produce some intellectually credible answers than just to give up and say the problem is too big and beyond a solution.

So, let's ask some of these questions about the causes of certain characteristics in our world and see if we can unravel clues to solve the seemingly endless mysteries that perplex us. These are the big problems that have exercised the minds of human beings from time immemorial. Since people began to stare into the night sky, the sense of wonder and the associated questions have been ever present. Where did we as a human race come from? Why are we here? What is the nature of ultimate reality? Is a natural or so-called 'scientific' analysis enough to help us solve the conundrum? Or do we need to look elsewhere?

I suspect, like me, you have often wondered about such things. It sometimes seems that there is no end to the issues calling for an explanation. Things that seem difficult to understand or categorise can be bothersome. The basic thesis here is that when we are regularly faced with an irritating enigma – we can take the logical approach, break it into more manageable chunks, apply the scientific method (or its close cousin in clinical medicine and surgery, the clinical method), then with the use of reason and some data we can often arrive at a solution. This is the way the clinical method works. It is the way the scientific method works.

First, let me tell a brief tale about an interchange in the late 19th century. This concerned an incident that will allow us to make an important link between reality and the underlying fundamental questions of causation or aetiology.

William James was an American philosopher and psychologist. Initially he trained as a physician and actually taught anatomy for some time at Harvard. He never did practise medicine but he became a leading psychologist. In fact, he published his highly respected, 1,200 page, two-volume work entitled the *The Principles of Psychology* back in 1890.

Dr. James was interested in making the scientific endeavour accessible to any who might be ready to listen. He was what we might call, a populariser of science. Reputedly, one day, when in a small American town, he gave a talk about the marvels of the solar system and had just finished explaining how the earth revolved around the sun, a fact that had been demonstrated at least three centuries earlier, when he apparently saw, according to the anecdote, an elderly lady approaching him with a determined look. She strongly disagreed, "This theory that the sun is the centre of the solar system", she said "and that the earth is a ball which rotates around it, while it has a very convincing ring to it, Mr. James, it's wrong. I've got a better explanation." So James politely responded, "And what is that, madam?" "Well," she said, "we live on a crust of earth which is settled on the back of a giant turtle." Not wishing to unkindly demolish this strange proposition with the volumes of scientific evidence which he undoubtedly had at his command, James decided to gently dissuade his inquisitor by helping her see some of the inadequacies of her position. "If your theory is correct, madam," he said, "what does this turtle stand on?" "Ah, Mr. James, that's a very good question, but I have an answer. And it's this: The first turtle stands on the back of a second, much larger turtle." "But what does this second turtle stand on?" persisted James patiently. To this, the lady announced triumphantly, "It's no use, Mr. James — it's turtles all the way down!" Without perhaps recognising what she had done, she had invoked what we might call an infinite regress. In fact, she expressed it rather well, "turtles all the way down."

Interpretations of the natural world that have enough explanatory power to be both correct and convincing are sometimes hard to find. As we encountered in our brief foray into the germ theory of putrefaction, even the correct answers did not land well in the scientific community. No wonder some scientists and clinicians are inclined to be cautious about launching their theories of cause and effect on an intolerant intellectual terrain.

Take home message ...

Identifying a causal explanation is a high ambition. Even when the problem seems out of reach, it is sensible to break it down into components and try to explain these to gain an insight into the overall conundrum.

Hesitant, nervous and unsure – but correct!

Threat is in the eye of the beholder.

Mohamed ElBaradei [1942-]

THE 16ᵀᴴ CENTURY WAS A heady time for scientific discovery. It was actually back in 1542 that the definitive publication giving William James his background authority on the topic of the solar system appeared. The author was rather nervous and concerned about how his challenging conclusions might be received. He was Nicolaus Copernicus [1473-1543]. Brought up in a religious family,

Monument to Nicolaus Copernicus with a compass and armillary sphere by Thorwaldsen, Warsaw.

it seemed his personal life attracted some scandal and a fair share of criticism. He was intellectually very gifted and matriculated in the University of Krakow in 1491 at the age of 18. He spoke several languages, was well grounded in the mathematical disciplines and developed a particular interest in astronomy. He became concerned at the contradictory nature of aspects of the conventional wisdom that had emerged from the two main competing systems of understanding, which, at that time, held sway over an appreciation of planetary movement.

At the beginning of the 16th century he developed some new skills in linguistics and also found time to take a medical course in Padua. However, his particular concern and the focus of much data collection in those years resulted in the completion, in 1532, of his famous work, *On the Revolutions of the Celestial Spheres*. News of his work gradually leaked but he was nervous about going into print because advancing a new idea such as this carried profound and far-reaching implications. So he did not publish for another 11 years. His view of cosmology placed the sun, not the earth, at the centre of the universe. Quite what his concern was, is now not so clear. Whether he was worried about the reception his work might have in the scientific and philosophical world or whether he was anxious about the reception in the religious realm is unknown. The book did finally appear just before he died in 1543. It triggered a revolution in astronomical thinking. As it turned out, he wasn't quite right about the exact nature of planetary orbits but there is no doubt that he had moved the argument in the right direction. That year, 1543, was the same year as another momentous and revolutionary publication – more of that later.

So, Copernicus was a reluctant visionary. He had knowingly thrown down a gauntlet to those who believed the traditional explanations were secure. Within the next 50 years or so, considerable interest in his work was generated by both Galileo Galilei [1564-1642] and Johannes Kepler [1571-1630]. Galileo was persuaded by the Copernican description of the circular orbits of planetary bodies but Kepler developed other ideas. While he was convinced by the heliocentric model of Copernicus, he was able to demonstrate that the planetary orbits were elliptical, not circular. At around that time, the use of the telescope became popular and made a huge difference to the ability to make accurate observations. So, good quality data challenged the time-honoured teaching and accepted dogma that had held sway for too long.

When the scientific community becomes persuaded about the veracity of an explanation, it is difficult and perhaps dangerous to challenge that position. It was ever thus. Even back in 1600, one unfortunate advocate of Copernicanism, Giordano Bruno, was burned at the stake. His crime? Not simply the view of heliocentrism or even the suggestions he made (again correctly) that distant stars were in some ways like the sun and were likely to be circled by other, perhaps even populated planets – his real crimes were that he disavowed church doctrine. Having non-mainstream scientific beliefs certainly didn't help.

Challenging the accepted belief system seemed (and still seems) to carry some risk. However, this is how scientific endeavour advances. It is by asking questions and challenging ideas, acquiring new data and fitting it all together; that is how we come to a refined and more accurate understanding of reality.

In the realm of medicine, there were some notable contributions made in anatomy and physiology at about the same time that the astronomers were trying to figure out how to make sense of their mathematics.

The classical teaching on human anatomy, even as recently as the 16th century, was based on the teachings of Galen [129-210]. He had been a prominent physician and philosopher in Greek society and had studied a range of medical theories. He was born in the town of Pergamon in Western Turkey and a bronze statue honouring his memory stands in the centre of the modern town of Bergama with the impressive backdrop of the ancient acropolis behind him.

As a young man, around 145AD, he studied for some four years in the nearby Asclepieion (these were ancient healing temples named after the legendary god of medicine, Asclepius). Galen then travelled around various cultural centres, including Alexandria, in the eastern Mediterranean. On his return to Pergamon he served as the chief physician to the gladiator school before moving to Rome where he spent the remainder of his life.

His appreciation of body structure and function was heavily influenced by the prior framework advanced by the teaching of Hippocrates [480 BC-370 BC] that the balance of the four humours, black bile, yellow bile, phlegm, and blood was essential to good health. Galen's anatomical understanding was actually based on animal anatomy, principally informed from the dissection of monkeys and pigs. Even when medical schools were set up in Europe in the 16th century, the anatomical teaching was Galenic and was handed down by Latin-speaking professors. On occasions, when rather less well-educated surgeons performed the human cadaveric dissection for teaching purposes, it is likely that attempts to demonstrate anatomical detail were totally lost on the audience, simply because the instructions would have been lost in translation!

It took a young, determined and talented Flemish surgeon and anatomist called Vesalius to displace the inaccurate Galenic teaching, which had such a stranglehold and replace it with careful observation, data collection, and reasoning. It was a real revolution in anatomical understanding. A scientific view of human anatomy had finally dawned and not before time!

Andreas Vesalius [1514-1564] was born in Brussels. He came from a medical family, studied medicine in Paris and, with the outbreak of war, ended up completing his studies in Padua. Vesalius was convinced that any surgical treatment had to be based on an accurate understanding of human anatomy. Rather surprisingly, when he competed his studies, he was so highly regarded that he was offered the chair of surgery and anatomy. His teaching style

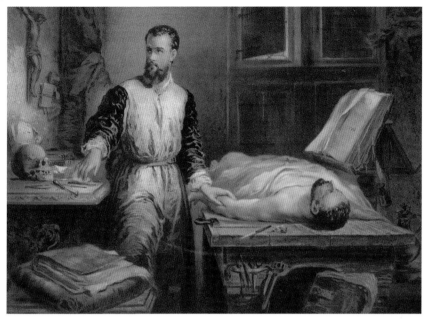

Andreas Vesalius at the dissecting table.
Artist Edouard Hamman [1819-1888].

was quite distinct in that he personally performed the dissections of human cadavers, making careful observations and records as he went along. When a local Paduan judge heard of his work and became interested, Vesalius soon had a secure supply of executed criminals!

Vesalius soon realised that Galen was wrong. It was perhaps risky to unseat the presiding paradigm but the truth was clear to him and he saw the importance of getting the record straightened out. In 1543, the same year that Copernicus produced his groundbreaking work; Vesalius published *De Humani Corporis Fabrica*. The book – all 700 pages of it, including some 200 exquisite illustrations, was based entirely on human dissection. It was, without doubt, the first truly scientific textbook of human anatomy. What is remarkable is that when it was published Vesalius was only 29 years old. He was a high achiever, of that there is no doubt, and he was also ambitious and sought a job as physician to the Holy Roman Emperor, Charles the

Fifth of Spain. Part of his application portfolio included a beautiful hand coloured copy of his *Fabrica*.

Vesalius challenged the accepted thinking which had prevailed for centuries and like so many others at around that time, (Copernicus [1473-1543], Harvey [1578-1657], Kepler [1571-1630]) produced paradigm shifts in scientific understanding. Heaving the scientific community in the appropriate direction required bravery, determination, and resilience. Revolutionary ideas, which don't quite fit the accepted dogma, always attract opposition. It is vital that details spoiling the fitness or logic of an accepted theory are not simply ignored, reinterpreted or explained away. Favoured or not, these 16th century luminaries were more interested in getting to the truth than in propping up a popular theory.

Ptolemy with his geocentric system of astronomy was popular but wrong. Galen with his classical understanding of anatomy was popular but wrong.

We must be careful not to assume or assert that our current understanding of reality has it all sewn up. There are many questions that emerge from data today that call into question some of the influential, popular, and accepted theories now endorsed in the 21st century. We will consider these enigmas here – and it will mean calling some of our beloved, default, and dogmatically-held ideas into question.

Take home message ...

Evidence is crucial. Even when the conclusions or implications run counter to the established consensus – following the evidence rather than being too concerned about upsetting sensitivities is the only logical route to progress.

A route to all the answers?

Judge a man by his questions rather than his answers.

Voltaire [1694-1778]

I HAVE ALWAYS BEEN PERSUADED that the scientific approach to understanding cause and effect is sensible, logical, and probably the most reliable way to discover anything significant about the natural world. It is inevitable that by its very nature, a scientific approach to a particular problem is likely to create as many questions as answers.

The objective in any scientific enterprise is to discover the truth about the natural world. It may relate to some basic and tightly controlled work in one of the pure sciences. Perhaps the most pure and *deductive* discipline would be mathematics and, indeed, it is arguably the only science in which genuine deductive conclusions can be drawn; conclusions that have the authority to carry the greatest degree of confidence. Alternatively, in the untidy business of working with data in biology or the clinical sciences, there are sometimes so many confounding variables, that these can be really tricky to disentangle in order to arrive at a secure conclusion. This is where the classical scientific method can be brought to the table.

There are various steps – all of them important, although some of them may seem to be self-evident or even take place on the fly. The approach to understanding a particular aspect of the natural world is usually based on an initial assessment or observation. The next step typically involves constructing a hypothesis to explain that observation. Quite frequently, the hypothesis will seek to suggest how the particular observation came to be – in essence a proposed cause for the observed reality. It is then important to consider how such a hypothesis might be put to the test – classically, an experimental design is set up to disprove the hypothesis. If such an attempt to falsify the hypothesis fails, then due consideration must be given to the level of confidence one can have in the conclusion that the hypothesis is correct. Sometimes it is important to tackle the question from a slightly different angle and apply some additional experimental data to add to that confidence. This entire activity is known as the *inductive* method of reasoning or investigation. Ultimately, if other workers can replicate and thus authenticate the results and conclusions, then there can be more general acceptance of a hypothesis.

The processes of *deductive* and *inductive* reasoning are philosophically rather different and it is important to appreciate that this can have an impact on the reliability of any conclusions that may be reached.

Deductive reasoning, on the one hand, works from the general to the more specific. It is the approach used to really test a conclusion. Starting with a general premise, it is often constructed with at least two related statements. If the two premises are correct, then the conclusion is the inevitable and logical outcome. If the premises are true, the conclusion is not in dispute.

With the *inductive* approach, the process is an attempt to move from specific observations, often attempting to recognise some patterns along the way and work towards more general conclusions. It may, for example, be an attempt to understand cause and effect. The conclusions are not as logically necessary as those reached by the deductive method. All one can say about accumulating inductive evidence is that the conclusion may be probable or highly probable, but unless there is a way of accounting for all possible evidence and every confounding variable, the conclusions will always be likely rather than certain. It is not really secure to jump from a set of particular observations and risk generalising, simply because, by definition, the generalisation cannot contain more detail than the sum of all the underlying particulars.

It is easy to see how the boundaries can be blurred between these two categories. In reality, elements of each are often used in an attempt to arrive at the truth. The rationale behind the scientific method essentially uses the more open-ended inductive approach, taking specific observations and making an attempt to generalise and derive a new means of explanation. While each technique comes at a problem from a different perspective they are both designed to help us arrive at a true and reliable understanding of reality.

There is a third approach that is often used and is rather different from either deduction or induction. It is sometimes known as 'abduction.' When there is no available, observable scientific data, one has to draw on experience and the way reality appears to behave in our usual appreciation of the world. This allows us to make an *inference to the best explanation*. This is really the only available route to a conclusion when there are gaps in the data. It may apply when there is no way of making real time observations and it is a matter of making the best impression we can from the limited data set available. In clinical science – when doctors try to make sense of a collection of symptoms, signs and laboratory results to arrive at a diagnosis, they almost always have to construct a list of possibilities; a list of plausible differential diagnoses and then weed out those possibilities which fail to provide the best fit for the accumulating data. At an early stage in the diagnostic process this might be likened to taking your best shot at a possible diagnosis and refining that as more and more information can be brought together. Thus, the abductive approach commonly applies when the data set is incomplete, either because the phenomena are historical and thus cannot be observed or are unobservable for other reasons.

The scientific method is tried and tested and applies to many disciplines. While it involves posing a particular question or tackling a specific problem, the end result may well build up a sophisticated body of knowledge and draw reliable conclusions. However, there are usually additional problems posed and additional factors that demand an explanation, so the process has to be revisited or repeated. It sometimes seems like the questions rarely reach an end-point - perplexity ad infinitum.

Let me introduce a slightly different angle to expose how scientists and clinicians often think. If we start with the realm of clinical science or human biology, we can ask questions, gain knowledge and unravel what appears to be most likely to explain some aspect of physical reality under study. This approach has a strong track record. It seems to offer the most promising prospect of a meaningful outcome and in simple terms, it involves reducing complex questions to their simplest components. This method is called *reductionism* and it comes in various guises.

It might be easiest to think of practical and theoretical versions of reductionism. Practically speaking, methodological reductionism involves the idea that complex biological systems should be investigated in terms of their molecular genetic, physiological or biochemical mechanisms. Breaking down complex metabolic pathways to their more basic chemical and physical mechanisms allows a granular and detailed understanding. This not only helps to explain why things are the way they are, but it opens up all sorts of further insights and opportunities. Reverse engineering a complex system not only provides a detailed understanding of how and why the components are so arranged and how they produce their particular effects, it can stimulate ideas in bio-mimetics, which is the idea that these same design principles can be applied in a completely different context.

From a purely philosophical angle, it is worth mentioning two other aspects of reductionism. The first of these is epistemic reductionism – the idea here is that the knowledge gained in one particular area can be best explained by a more basic discipline. For example, an attempt to explain control mechanisms in the circulation might include an investigation of the physiological control of blood pressure, which in turn might be best explained by the biochemical effects of various hormones which, again, in turn are active at the more fundamental level of simpler vasoactive signaling and control molecules. The characteristics of these can then be further investigated by breaking them down to the more basic details of chemistry and physics. It will be immediately recognised that there is a link between the theoretical and practical aspects of reductionism – this epistemic variety is closely related to the description of methodological reductionism.

A slightly different philosophical take exposes an important assumption and this is based on the notion of ontological reductionism. Here, the idea is that any biological system can be understood in terms of nothing more than the physical characteristics and interactions of the constituent atoms and molecules. Philosophically, this is sometimes known as physicalism or materialism. Despite the fact there are aspects of life and consciousness that don't easily fit into such a model, this approach would probably be the reigning paradigm that governs thinking about biological reality. It asserts, of course, that pretty much every aspect of life can be explained in purely physical terms. At first blush this may seem uncontroversial. It is when one asks the more detailed questions that all sorts of perplexing inconsistencies emerge and the puzzles mount up.

So, let's chase this reductionist idea a little further. Could it be that the basic scientific methodologies can provide answers to every question about the physical and biological world? A few significant and highly respected individuals certainly appear (or appeared) to think so.

Take this excerpt from the writing of chemistry professor, Peter Atkins FRSC (b 1940]. Atkins is a British chemist and former Professor of Chemistry at the University of Oxford and a Fellow of Lincoln College. He is well known as an author of popular chemistry textbooks and other works including *Galileo's Finger*. His conviction is that the scientific endeavour is omni-competent with respect to its explanatory power.

'Science, the system of belief founded securely on publicly shared reproducible knowledge, emerged from religion. As science discarded its chrysalis to become its present butterfly, it took over the heath. *There is no reason to suppose that science cannot deal with every aspect of existence.* Only the religious - among whom I include not only the prejudiced but the uninformed - hope there is a dark corner of the physical universe, or of the universe of experience, that science can never hope to illuminate. But science has never encountered a barrier, and *the only grounds for supposing that reductionism will fail are pessimism on the part of scientists and fear in the minds of the religious.*"[7]

Here is another example from a highly rated philosopher, logician, writer, social activist, and winner of the Nobel Prize for literature - Bertrand Russell [1872 1970]. "Science, in its ultimate ideal, consists of a set of propositions arranged in a hierarchy, the lowest level of the hierarchy being concerned with particular facts, and the highest with some general law, governing everything in the universe. The various levels in the hierarchy have a two-fold logical connection, travelling one up, one down; the upward connection proceeds by induction, the downward by deduction."[8]

Bertrand Russell
[1872-1970]

"I conclude that, while it is true that science cannot decide questions of value, that is because they cannot be intellectually decided at all, and lie outside the realm of truth and falsehood. *Whatever knowledge is attainable, must be attained by scientific methods; and what science cannot discover, mankind cannot know.*"[9]

Without doubt Bertrand Russell had a formidable intellect. Here, he made the link between questions and the methodology used to address them. Unfortunately, his logic misfired when he made that statement. This is an example of a philosophically incoherent paradox, claiming as it does that only scientific methods can result in true knowledge. This statement is clearly not derived from any scientific enquiry, so by reference to itself – it cannot be trusted. It is self-referentially incoherent; a bit like making the claim that there is no such thing as absolute truth! The best example I know of a self-referentially incoherent statement is sometimes used as an example of the 'liar paradox,' and it runs like this: 'This statement is false.' It is a contradiction – it is tantamount to claiming that 'A' is 'not A' so is logically incoherent.

Science then, whether or not we can pick apart issues in the underlying philosophy or language, does appear in the minds of some to assume huge explanatory power. One is left to wonder whether there is actually a definable limit to its reach.

Take home message …

Reductionism, while a highly popular component of the scientific method, can be a constraint if certain classes of viable explanation are ruled out. The result can lead to illogical and self-defeating conclusions.

Are there issues that science just cannot explain?

There ain't no answer. There ain't gonna be any answer. There never has been an answer. That's the answer.

Gertrude Stein [1874-1946]

ANOTHER VERY GIFTED AND HIGHLY regarded scientist also had some perceptive observations to make on the possible limits which may apply to the extent to which the scientific method can address perplexing questions. Peter Medawar [1915-1987] became famous for his work on tissue immunology.

Sir Peter Medawar
[1915-1987]

Indeed, in 1960 he jointly won the Nobel Prize for Physiology and Medicine for his description of acquired immune tolerance. Much of the more important and fundamental work was carried out in Glasgow. He spent some time there working in collaboration with a prominent plastic surgeon called Tom Gibson.

Gibson had been working on skin grafting and he and Medawar described the 'second set' phenomenon which really laid the foundations for transplantation surgery. They published their famous paper in the *Journal of Anatomy* in July 1943. So vital was that work to the subsequent unravelling of immune tolerance that Medawar wrote to Gibson thanking him for the insight into the 'real problem' that they faced as they worked on their research question together. Medawar went on to hold senior academic posts in Birmingham and London and was well known as a gifted writer with a notable sense of both perception and humour. In his little book *The Limits of Science*[10] he makes a couple of interesting observations. In the abstract of his central essay he notes that the view held in the seventeenth century failed to recognise a limit to science. He goes on to point out, "The existence of a limit to science is, however, made clear by its inability to answer childlike elementary questions having to do with first and last things – questions such as 'How did everything begin?'; 'What are we all here for?'; 'What is the point of living?'" He indicates that his purpose is simply to 'exculpate' science, which is a glorious and successful enterprise, from the reproach that it is quite unable to answer those ultimate questions. Nor should we expect science to answer all such questions just as it would be futile to 'reproach a railway locomotive for not flying or, in general, not performing any other operation for which it is not designed.'

There was a major political spat in London towards the end of 2009. This concerned the sacking of a very eminent psycho-pharmacologist who had been the Chairman of the UK Government's Advisory Committee on the Misuse of Drugs since 1998. Professor David Nutt was an academic at the University of Bristol at that time. In 2007 he published a controversial study on the harms of drug use and, as a result, he repeatedly clashed with government ministers and it eventually led to his dismissal from his advisory role to the government. He was perceived to be both a government adviser and a campaigner against government policy. Alan Johnson, a Labour politician and the Home Secretary at the time, sacked him and there was a huge outcry. The reaction was extensively covered in the broadcast media and in early November 2009 an announcer (Justin Webb) on the BBC Radio Four flagship news and current affairs Today programme introduced the item with this statement: "Science – the very word conjures up, in the modern mind, a sense of trustworthiness and respect for rational truth."

It seemed like a very reasonable and accurate assessment of the way science is viewed by the general public. It was put in perspective by another contributor to the 'World this Weekend' (a BBC current affairs programme) on November 1st. Lord Robert Winston, a well-known infertility researcher, broadcaster and populariser of science was interviewed and offered this analysis: "Science is not about certainty. Science is about probability. Science is not about absolutes. We scientists give the impression that science is about the truth. It's not! It's about what is most likely."

This was an excellent description of the limitation of the inductive reasoning that underpins so much of scientific enquiry.

I am convinced that Medawar was right. There is a clear limit to the kind of questions that can be answered scientifically. Science is very useful in any exploration of how the world works. It has little or even nothing to contribute to the related questions that begin with 'Why.' The perplexing questions children ask. The ultimate questions of Karl Popper, articulated by Medawar. Why is the world the way it is? Why does the universe exist? What is the purpose of living? What is the nature of ultimate reality?

It is worth listing at least five categories where science is quite unable, or even unsuited, to make a meaningful contribution. While that may be the case, it is nevertheless perfectly reasonable and rational to hold securely to the knowledge we may have about these subjects and to rely on the rationality that underpins that knowledge. Here we go.

First, when you think about it, science is completely dependent on a system of reasoning and analysis and so has to assume that the laws of logic are both sound and reliable and also that mathematical analysis can be trusted. There is no sense in which science can verify either of these categories. One just has to accept that it is entirely reasonable and proper to trust the various components with which we have become so familiar – we don't even pause to doubt their reliability but there is no scientific way to prove that reliability. Indeed, to try to prove these factors scientifically would require us to argue in a circle; we'd have to try to prove the conclusion that logic and mathematics were secure by using the very principles of logic and maths! Circular reasoning, of course, is one classic form of logical fallacy.

Secondly, we would struggle to find a scientific basis for issues of morality. It is not at all unusual for people to have an acute awareness of moral principles; issues such as fairness or professional ethical standards that we expect of, for example, doctors or lawyers or indeed any profession or business. To ground an understanding of the way things ought to be requires a system of ethics or values and these are not verified by any of the mechanisms of scientific methodology. So that is another area for which the provenance appears to be completely separated from a scientific basis.

Actually, there is more, much more. Indeed as I think about it, some of the most precious experiences of life fall into categories that exist beyond the scientific endeavour. Take our third category as an illustration of this. Consider the satisfaction we experience from art or music. The appreciation and enjoyment that can be derived from a good novel, a well-struck topspin drive on the tennis court, or a solid long straight tee shot on the golf course. For sure we can understand some elements of the physical properties of colour, sound or motion but the abstract, peculiar and specific aesthetic sense of pleasure or excitement that these various elements of style or beauty can produce is not open to scientific enquiry. Just because these abstract features cannot be subjected to the scientific approach does nothing to devalue their reality or importance.

How about that strange family of difficult issues that are sometimes grouped as metaphysical questions? Are they amenable to scientific answers? Again, it looks like this area is beyond the scope of natural science, on account of the very nature of the questions that can be grouped under this heading. These would include the fundamental questions about the true nature of reality, questions of origin or meaning; where did we come from? What is the purpose of life? These are the questions of a child, which Sir Peter Medawar mentioned. What about the nature and origin of intelligence or free will? Could there be a parallel reality to the reality we think we observe? Is there any sense in which inanimate things behave? All of these questions are reasonable enough but there is no sense in which a scientific enquiry can probe far enough to lead to any satisfactory conclusions.

The final category I want to mention here reminds me of the incoherent proposition of Bertrand Russell that we considered earlier. "*Whatever knowledge is attainable, must be attained by scientific methods; and what science cannot discover, mankind cannot know.*" We saw already that from a philosophical point of view, that statement, if true, really self-destructs! But think about this – never mind the nondescript catch all "whatever knowledge" idea - instead apply it to 'science' itself and ask the question, 'Is it possible to provide scientific justification for science?' As it turns out, with a moment's thought it will become clear that, oddly enough, even science itself, as a venture, cannot be justified by any scientific method.

We already saw the importance of reasoning and a system of numerical analysis to allow us to derive any conclusions from observations we make, but there is at least another assumption we are obliged to make for scientific activity to work. We presume that the natural world is going to behave pretty much in the orderly and predictable way we have seen it behave before. It is certainly reasonable to assume that because our repeated experience of some aspect of the natural world has been a regular, orderly and consistent experience, it is clearly not risky to assume that in the future things will continue to behave as we have seen them behave before. However, we cannot necessarily guarantee that this will be the case. Just because the future has been like the past in the past, does not guarantee that the future will be like the past in the future! To try to insist that it will, cannot be proved scientifically. We would be guilty of simply assuming the very position that needs to be proved scientifically, and thus find ourselves trapped again by arguing in a circle. So even the scientific lab coat is not hung on a secure scientific peg!

It is sensible at this point to introduce a new term. There is no doubt whatsoever about the usefulness of science, but we have to recognise its limits and the various areas where it just cannot reach or really apply. So, those who continue to maintain or claim that the only way really to know something requires proof from the hard sciences, find themselves clinging to a belief that is not justifiable. It is not science, it is *scientism*!

Making sense of the kind of assumptions that science can justifiably make is not a scientific exercise but rather an issue for philosophy. Science is not about truth, it is about what is most likely, it's about probability. Scientism is damaging to science; it gives a false impression about what science can actually achieve and it undermines and misrepresents the assumptions that a scientist can make. While science can do so much, it falls short of some of the most perplexing conundrums and is simply not fit for the purpose of fully addressing them. This is ironically all the more obvious when its reach for truth is confined to the tools of physical science. To go beyond the naturalistic sciences and consider the perfectly rational conclusion that there may be evidence of design in nature, of necessity, goes beyond naturalism and infers a designing agency, which is beyond the bounds of scientific analysis and so is automatically ruled out of court. It is such a shame that while the scientific method purports to lead to a truthful understanding of the world, as we have seen, so much of the important stuff is beyond the reach of scientific methodology and so is debarred. Confining our enquiry to the terms imposed by methodological naturalism excludes a tract of analysis wherein the real truth may lie, because we disallow consideration of an approach that could lead to an accurate understanding of the big questions of nature. Maybe the apparent design in biology is not an illusion. If the design is real, it would be a shame to shield our view by wearing scientific blinkers. What we need is a true and justified understanding, even if it is not considered, in the minds of some, to be science.

Take home message ...

Assuming that science can provide answers to every question is clearly incorrect and to adhere to that view is not science – it is a fallacy; 'scientism.'

It is all about knowing - Epistemology

The urge to know scrapes against the inability to know.

Anthony Doerr [1973-]

THE IDEA THAT THE TOOLS of science must be restricted to physical or natural observable factors – so-called methodological naturalism – gets in the way of the possibility that there are other ways to know things. The scientific method is sometimes categorised as empiricism. It is, however, perfectly rational to rely on other ways of making sense of the world in an attempt to reach an accurate understanding about what is really true. To reject, up front, that there are other epistemological tools (methods, validity and scope of arriving at a state of knowing something) available as a means of arriving at secure knowledge, binds our thinking quite unnecessarily. Of course, observation and the use of sense perception are key components, but so are the tools of logical and rational analysis. Intuition, and authority can also play a part. So how can we assess whether we have arrived at the truth in any situation? When answering a question or solving a scientific conundrum, the usual assessments of truth are employed without thinking too deeply about them. They include such considerations as logical consistency. We also like to make sure that we don't overcomplicate our explanations, so we opt for the simplest and most straightforward explanation

73

when presented with a set of alternatives. If an explanation becomes so elaborate or perhaps unnecessarily complicated, we naturally begin to suspect the conclusion and, of course, any answer needs to be specifically relevant to the question itself.

For some people the pursuit of truth is a dogged affair and there is no guarantee of a satisfactory outcome. Here again we encounter our friend (this time the fictitious Baron) Münchausen whose name is associated with a thought experiment, the Münchausen trilemma,[11] which technically purports to outline the impossibility of ever arriving at the truth of any proposition.

Probably the signature tale which might explain the connection with our imaginary Baron is the story in which the braggart is said to have pulled himself and his horse from a swamp by dragging himself upwards by his own hair; the ultimate boot-strapping trick! One part of the trilemma requires proof of the proof, ad absurdum (remember the turtles?). Another part is based on a trust in certain accepted underlying principles or assumptions upon which the proof is based and the final element recalls the notion of circularity where the question and answer both rely on one another. It is, however, one of a number of philosophical ideas, the like of which we have encountered before, where no matter how you look at the claim, it fails its own test – what indeed is the proof that the options in the trilemma itself are proved? It is rather like the statement, "There is no such thing as absolute truth"; if it's true, it's false and if it's false, it's false. Self-refuting statements are always false!

I have come to the conclusion that there has often been serious ideological interference in the matter of sorting truth from science and it needs attention to detail. It is important, therefore, to carefully evaluate the nature of any conclusion in the light of the under-pinning evidence and to consider the source, volume, reliability, authenticity, and credibility of that evidence. The falsifiability of the evidence is also relevant. It is important to establish if the conclusion can be verified and considered true, or whether it would be safer either to hold it provisionally or even discard it altogether.

We also need to be aware that scientists will frequently, and sometimes simply as a matter of course rather than as a premeditated move, overlay their reasoning with a set of philosophical assumptions or prejudices. These can contaminate the language they may use to describe or interpret the findings or the conclusions they may wish to draw. I suppose we might regard that as a kind of scientific spin. The danger is the temptation to think within a framework which, by its nature, can lead to describing findings in a way which bows to some a priori assumptions or assertions which themselves are difficult to genuinely justify. Indeed, such pre-suppositional assumptions may be perfectly credible in themselves. However, no matter how popular or commonly held they may be, it is far more important that they are really justified because of the possible subliminal effect they may have on the take home message.

This is exactly how spin works in the political sphere. We are exposed to it all the time. The term became particularly well known in the UK during the premiership of Tony Blair (he was British Prime Minister from 1997-2007). His administration became known for the way in which it presented information to the media. One of the key figures in the communication of the Labour Party at that time was Alastair Campbell. His background was in journalism, but he became Blair's campaign director and spokesman before the 1997 general election and thereafter was the Downing Street Director of Communications. During that time he was seen as the architect of a formidable and effective apparatus for ensuring that there was a high degree of control over the timing and content of any message that was broadcast or published. He was one of the most effective spin-doctors of his time and the importance of controlling information about any issue in politics or commerce is now seen to be of great importance. Many large companies and organisations now have individuals or even whole departments driven by the objective of packaging exactly the right message, with the right language in the right form and at the right time. There are numerous techniques that can be used to convincing effect. Selectively presenting only certain facts will sometimes put a particular gloss on a story or message. This is deliberately deployed to convey an untrue account of some situation without actually resorting to the communication of a technical untruth. It is a matter of telling only part of a story; being economical with the truth. It is a form of manipulation of opinion or of propaganda and the bottom line is that it is misleading. One of the best descriptions I came across in reading about this came from the memoirs of Marlin Fitzwater which he published in an entertaining book, *Call the Briefing*, about his time as White House Press Secretary during the Reagan and Bush years.[12] His definition is interesting – spin is the "weaving of a thread of truth into the fabric of a lie." The result can be appealing, convincing, persuasive, and *wrong*! The selective accumulation of information to support a particular position, the clever subliminal effects of a carefully chosen analogy and even the sentence construction can disguise a correct interpretation of reality.

In science reporting, this can be a way of dictating the discussion towards only a particular kind of conclusion. In a search for an accurate understanding of reality we must be alert to spin. We ought to be ready to ask if there is a subtext or hidden agenda, or even a set of assumptions which rule out a perfectly reasonable alternative explanation. We must bring the factual sources into the open and we must also be ready to use our common sense and logic, even if that is the only way to provide a bridge for a gap in the data. Please note that I am not suggesting for one moment that we may have to simply give up the attempt to understand or reach the answer to some difficult question. I do not subscribe to a 'god of the gaps' or a 'science of the gaps' approach, just because we don't yet fully understand something. In fact, come to think about it, there are some areas that may actually, genuinely, be beyond our capacity to resolve. But more of that later.

For now, let me take you back to the clinical realm. There, we have numerous scientific conundrums to consider. In tackling them we will give the scientific approach its rightful place and together with the clinical method see what sense we can make of some interesting mysteries.

We can certainly celebrate the successes of the clinical and scientific method, but it is also important to show its limitations. Not everything is reducible to the basics of physiology, the molecular machinery, or even more basic sciences such as physics and chemistry.

Take home message ...

Even the use of a reliable evidence based method is subject to interpretation and scientific 'spin' such that the resulting conclusions and implications are off target.

Clinical Conundrum: The importance of determining cause

> *Medicine is a science of uncertainty and an art of probability.*
>
> William Osler [1849-1919]

I HAD BEEN LEARNING THE SCIENCE and craft of clinical surgery for years and yet had never come across the term 'medical semiology'. It sounded like some kind of specialty – but what? I have since learned that there are courses in medical schools all over the world on clinical semiotics. When I first heard the term and learned that it was a very basic and fundamental part of clinical medicine, I was just a little concerned. It was a closed book to me and I was already qualified. How could this be? As it turned out, I was unwittingly already well versed in the art and practice of semiology – I had just never come across the term. It has to do with the business of interpreting a patient's symptoms and signs. This relies, first and foremost, on what is known as the clinical method. This is a means of understanding the patient and addressing the detail of his or her presentation and of understanding their disease or problem. The mainstays of the successful use of the clinical method need both a thorough problem-oriented history of the illness – that is an account of what the symptoms are, or the story of how these have developed since they started - and a careful physical (or psychological) examination. It is amazing that you can often get quite close to a final diagnosis just by the use of a skillfully-taken history. Having initially assessed the patient, it is usually possible to construct a list of possible diagnoses – so-called differential diagnoses. Ordering these by which is most likely can then help to dictate which bedside, laboratory or imaging investigations may help resolve the conundrum. It is always the intention to be objective and rational although admittedly, just as in other branches of science, what the results could mean will often depend on how they are interpreted. This is probably the weakest part of the entire process. Doctors can make errors of interpretation in lots of different ways. For example, it is well known that there is a tendency to rely too heavily on the first item of information or the first indication that there is support from a laboratory test leading to premature closure, or jumping to a conclusion by introducing a form of cognitive bias. There is also a tendency for groups of doctors to refer to patients, not by name, but by a suitable label, for example, 'the bleeder', the 'biliary sepsis', or the 'pneumonia' - a sure way to introduce mistakes from time to time.

While laboratory results and imaging studies go a long way to objectify the data, doctors are always less accurate because many subjective components can confound a clinical presentation. Even the patient may be inclined to spin particular symptoms or signs that matter more to them and their understanding, concerns, expectations, hopes, and feelings also enter the fray. In the same way, a clinician's subjective overlay should not confound the process. Such an objective process runs into difficulty when the actual cause of the malady is functional or not demonstrably physical or even properly psychological.

I will never forget such a case that caused me some angst as a fourth year medical student. During my undergraduate attachment in psychological medicine, I was required to write a detailed report on a particular case. It was my misfortune to be assigned a rather sensitive, almost notorious, case and one I will never forget. I was given an address and asked to visit a family where there was a range of psychiatric morbidity. It was a desperately sad situation. The trigger was an infamous murder case in Glasgow that became known as the Golspie Street murders.[13]

In January of 1976 there was one remaining occupied apartment in a tenement building in Govan, at that time a particularly run-down and deprived part of Glasgow, not far from the city centre. A redevelopment programme for that part of the city was underway and the one family who remained in the decaying building faced regular threats from vandals and vagrants. A brother and sister aged 12 and 13 had been left alone in the house whilst the father and another daughter of the family were out. When they returned they made the macabre discovery of the bodies of the two children, bound, gagged, and horribly beaten to death. Senior detectives described the scene as possibly the most brutal they had ever seen. My patient was a close relative of the two murdered children. On the night of the funerals, having been previously well, she suddenly developed loss of sensation and movement in her legs. This was dramatic and, by the time I went to visit her, she had already been in a wheelchair and quite unable to walk for several months. A careful history linked the onset of these catastrophic symptoms to the acute stress of the murders and detailed clinical examination revealed that there was likely no physical cause for her symptoms. In some ways, similar to the doctor deception of Münchausen-like behaviour, she appeared to have deceived herself with a clinical syndrome that just did not fit with any physical ailment. The telltale signs gave it away. If someone had a loss of motor function and sensation at a particular level of say the spinal cord, the pattern of nerve distribution is so well known anatomically that it is possible to map it very accurately to the exact site of the lesion. In this case, rather than conforming to the anatomical segments, the sensory loss involved everything below a horizontal band at the level of her waist (which would have been around the level of the 8th thoracic vertebra); her motor loss did not correspond. If she had a physical lesion or damage to her spinal cord at that level, she would have had impairment of muscle function in her chest and would likely have suffered from major difficulty in controlling bowel and bladder function. This particular patient may already have had some risk factors even before the trigger of the murder case – there was a background of anxiety and a history of depression and her own children had major problems with vision because of a congenital birth defect. It is thought that such additional factors as these may have augmented the psychological stress response and such factors are not uncommon in cases like this. This case was another example of a factitious disorder. In those days we referred to it as conversion hysteria, or hysterical paralysis, but that name has been rather outlawed now.

When all is said and done, and while we can recognise some patterns in cases like this, it is easy to arrive at an incorrect diagnosis and perhaps ascribe the problem to some dreaded physical condition. It serves to illustrate the importance of a carefully deployed clinical method to get close to the truth. We may well be curious as to why on earth psychological or factitious disorders like this occur. Clearly, if we really understood the cause we would be better placed to offer specific therapy, rather than the supportive and rather non-specific treatment that is about all that is really available. Understanding the aetiology or cause of a condition often allows an in-depth assessment of what is really going on. The frustrating thing is that so often making such a determination can generate as many further questions as it does answers.

Perplexing as cases like mine can be, the reality of clinical practice is that we are surrounded by patients for whom we have little more than a sketchy appreciation of the cause of their maladies. Doctors have a habit of using labels and technical language that tends to give the impression that we mostly know what we are talking about. Digging under the surface can sometimes give a very different impression!

Clinical medicine is full of unexplained phenomena. Puzzling scenarios, suites of features that don't quite fit or can't be easily explained. Sometimes they even seem to run so counter to accepted orthodoxy that it is hard to know where to start. The end result, of course, is that many more questions than answers emerge. If only these clinical problems were readily reducible to the fundamental principles of biochemistry, physiology, and pathology, we might have a better handle on how to manage them.

Modern medicine has made dramatic strides. Our ability to make refined diagnoses and offer personalised treatment is one of the most encouraging and thrilling advances of the past few years – so-called precision medicine. For the future, we can envisage a time when an individual's diagnosis will be made with uncanny accuracy; sophisticated imaging and the application of genetic and modern molecular techniques will help to classify the individual genome, proteome, and metabolome, such that we not only have a clear understanding of the cause of a particular problem, but we can characterise it in detail and define exactly the right treatment option from the menu of available therapies.

For now, however, there are still many clinical conditions that are a puzzle. Let me lead you through a few examples.

Take home message ...

At a practical level, many aspects of clinical medicine may appear to be well understood. The whole enterprise is peppered with assumptions and unanswered questions.

Wondering why

Men go abroad to wonder at the heights of mountains, at the huge waves of the sea, at the long courses of the rivers, at the vast compass of the ocean, at the circular motions of the stars, and they pass by themselves without wondering.

Augustine [354-430]

"DAD, DO YOU EVER WONDER about things?" So ran the question from my eight-year-old daughter. Her consistent experience was that I had answers to all the puzzling constituents of her life, so her question was quite legitimate. In fact, as her interest in reading grew to such an extent that she went on to study English literature, there is no doubt that her knowledge diverged from and eclipsed her father's quite quickly.

The story is told of the legendary Dr. Samuel Johnson who was visiting a friend with an impressive collection of art as well an extensive library. Johnson had been born in 1709 and various disabling and threatening illnesses had punctuated his childhood. It is a testimony to his considerable resilience that he bore all of that with some fortitude.

His father had a bookstore and it is no surprise that, as a child, Johnson was an avid reader. He became a student at Oxford but was in no position to service the financial commitment which that entailed, so despite his extensive learning and formidable intellect, he had to give up and he dabbled in teaching before developing a career as an accomplished writer, poet, essayist and literary critic. Whilst in his fifties he made the acquaintance of a young Scotsman named James Boswell and Boswell made extensive notes of their conversations together and ended up writing the celebrated biography – 'The Life of Samuel Johnson.' In 1775 when the two friends were guests along with the famous artist, Sir Joshua Reynolds, their host was curious as to the reason Johnson seemed to spend so much time in the library and why he appeared to take such an intense interest in the book collection. At that point he apparently uttered the statement about knowledge that has become one of his more famous quotations. The relevant section of Boswell's writing is well worth reviewing. The paragraph reads: "No sooner had we made our bow to Mr. Cambridge in his library, than Johnson ran eagerly to one side of the room, intent on poring over the backs of the books. Sir Joshua observed, (aside,) 'He runs to the books, as I do to the pictures: but I have the advantage. I can see much more of the pictures than he can of the books.' Mr. Cambridge, upon this, politely said, 'Dr. Johnson, I am going, with your pardon, to accuse myself, for I have the same custom which I perceive you have. But it seems odd that one should have such a desire to look at the backs of books.' Johnson, ever ready for contest, instantly started from his reverie, wheeled about, and answered, 'Sir, the reason is very plain. Knowledge is of two kinds. We know a subject ourselves, or we know where we can find information upon it. When we enquire into any subject, the first thing we have to do is to know what books have treated of it. This leads us to look at catalogues, and the backs of books in libraries.' Sir Joshua observed to me the extraordinary promptitude with which Johnson flew upon an argument. 'Yes, (said I,) he has no formal preparation, no flourishing with his sword; he is through your body in an instant.'"[14]

In our generation, it is rare to see writing of such quality, but the claim still applies – in fact one danger is that we tend to rely more and more on the search engines to service the second category of knowledge, such that we may be in danger of allowing Johnson's primary category to dwindle!

PUZZLING DIAGNOSES

Despite our extensive and accumulated knowledge reserves, whether cerebral or digital, there are still plenty of things that just don't quite make sense. In clinical medicine, and this is far from reassuring for a non-medical readership, it is easy to think of illnesses about which very little is known, especially when it comes to understanding the origin of particular conditions. We can describe but we struggle to understand how these suites of symptoms and signs come together. We can give them fancy names but a name frequently belies the fact that the underlying causes or even perhaps the mechanism or pathophysiology remain a mystery.

For some, the problem relates exactly to the lack of any confident understanding of a cause, while for others, the mechanism is the mystery. For still others there is no good treatment. There are some examples where we have an inkling about cause, we may even understand what is called the pathophysiology, yet it is the curious and inconsistent way the diagnosis behaves in different individuals that causes the puzzle. Let me give you some examples of each of these.

Ask any doctor, for example, to explain cluster headaches. You are likely to get a blank stare. These are awful. Admittedly they generally don't last for that long, nevertheless the pain can be excruciating, disabling even, and there are sometimes some visible signs, a watery red eye, a droopy eyelid, and maybe even inequality in the sizes of the pupils. Some of the more adventurous medics might well come out with a convincing sounding story, but in reality any story that is told does not come from a secure base and is likely speculative at best. Sure, there is a vague notion that there may be some kind of link to smoking and drinking, but that is about as far as any connection to causation goes. We just do not know why these nasty pains occur.

Or how about the curious and anomalous condition, not very savoury, I realise, known as the solitary rectal ulcer syndrome (SRUS)? This is a troublesome and annoying condition for which any convincing explanation of its cause leaves one feeling that it is really hard to be sure. There are some reasonable explanations that could possibly apply, but equally, it might also be that the surgeons and physiologists who try to explain this are really making the best of what amounts to circumstantial evidence. Is it related to intra-abdominal pressure, inappropriate muscle contraction, or bowel habit? All of these have been postulated to play a part. Even the condition itself can take different forms and while there are some characteristic features, which are typical of SRUS when biopsies are examined under the microscope, the reality is that many aspects of this curious and unpleasant condition remain a mystery.

There is a veritable host of conditions that share these enigmatic characteristics. Neuralgia is another diagnostic label that conceals a vast gap in our understanding. Doctors have this bad habit of using their own unique language and that includes giving things names which often sound like explanations but in reality are little more than descriptions. Neuralgia is a case in point. The origin of the term is from the Greek words for nerve and for pain and to be honest, for many forms of neuralgia, that it is nerve related pain is about as much as we know about it. We can make it sound even more enigmatic of course by identifying the likely associated nerve as in trigeminal neuralgia, occipital neuralgia, and even glossopharyngeal neuralgia. Sometimes there is a good explanation for nerve related pain as can happen when an intervertebral disc prolapses in the lower spine resulting in direct pressure on a nerve root, often producing pain and sensory loss over the distribution of the sciatic nerve – hence 'sciatica' but, as for many of these other varieties, while there are all sorts of theories, no one is terribly sure why the pain occurs.

Come to think of it, I am now not sure that Johnson and Boswell's classification of knowledge is comprehensive enough for these clinical mysteries. Having the knowledge about something or knowing how to find it out may be all well and good. The reality is that there has to be an additional category. Some things just continue to remain unknown.

Tales of medical discovery can be intriguing. Sometimes the story is the result of painstaking and logical investigation. Not infrequently, however, significant advances result from an assortment of accidental observations, or having the key people with relevant experience or awareness being in the right place and at the right time. This certainly applies across many clinical disciplines. From the unravelling of surgical antisepsis, the discovery of anaesthesia, the recognition of the effects of various drugs including some antibiotics (notably penicillin), some psychoactive drugs and, amongst many others, even the discovery of insulin. We'll pick up at least one of these stories later when we have a look at certain enigmatic aspects of neuroscience.

And then, there is a family of unrelated conditions. While that sounds like a contradiction, it is nevertheless the case that while these perplexing problems are not related by site, system, physiological effects, symptoms, or signs, they are all nevertheless linked because they are all idiopathic.

Anything that is 'idiopathic' is part of this family. Anything idiopathic is, by definition, enigmatic – we just don't yet understand it. Some of the idiopathic family has been the subject of study for generations and yet we are no closer to understanding the relevant cause. There is great diversity within this group of conditions. We have, for example, idiopathic oedema where there is unexplained swelling of the limbs, usually the legs, and it can be fiendishly difficult to treat. There is acute idiopathic polyneuritis, idiopathic skeletal hyperostosis, idiopathic pulmonary fibrosis, idiopathic scoliosis, - the list goes on and the puzzles pile up.

To break things up a little, doctors have found other words (another example of the tendency I mentioned already) for conditions that in reality are idiopathic but are not labelled as such. Sometimes terms like 'essential' or 'cryptogenic' are used instead. We have, for example, 'essential hypertension' – high blood pressure for a reason that no one can really articulate. Sure, there are some theories but that is about as far as it goes. Or how about cryptogenic cirrhosis, where the liver tissue becomes scarred and rigid and not only progressively loses the ability to work the metabolic miracles it has to work on a daily basis, it also causes all sorts of additional problems by messing with the local circulation, the so-called portal circulation. And when that gets screwed up, all manner of other problems can arise. One fact about this particular diagnosis is that we can confidently say what doesn't explain it. Cirrhosis can result from various viruses or the effects of alcohol but these just do not apply to the cryptogenic cases. While it is now thought that many of these cases might relate to what is known as steatosis or fatty liver disease, there is still a remnant that remains a mystery. In all these diseases, it pretty much comes to the same thing – we haven't much of a clue as to why they occur, what the cause is and sometimes, while we can recognise the syndromes or patterns of linked symptoms and physical signs, the members of the idiopathic family remain as mysterious as ever.

Curious Cancers

There is a curious and often dangerous type of tumour called a neuroblastoma. To understand its tissue of origin we need a quick excursion into the amazing organisation and development of the human nervous system. The central nervous system is a main command and control centre for everything that happens in human physiology or psychology. Clearly the brain and the associated peripheral network of nerves are responsible for this regulation. Just about everything we do as a result of voluntary action is the responsibility of the division that is called the somatic nervous system. However, consider this, just about everything else, that is all the processes responsible for keeping us alive, are never even a consideration at conscious level. These behave as an incredibly complex automated process. So the rate at which our heart beats or how deeply and how frequently we breathe, how our digestive system operates, how active various tissues are, how metabolism is controlled, how the inter-related endocrine organs work, control of oxygen delivery, blood pressure and blood production, how we respond to stress or injury, wound healing, and so on; all of these areas are primarily automatic and it is the autonomic nervous system which deals with all that activity. We never give a second thought to how intense the secretion of digestive enzymes has to be to deal with the fish and chips we have just consumed, or how much bile to mobilise from the store in the gall bladder to help cope with the fat content of that intake. We don't get involved in any of the essential and vital components of the inflammatory or metabolic responses to injury or invasion, but the autonomic system, together with a system of chemical messengers, is instantly active, controlling, measuring, adjusting, feeding detail back to the central control tower and refining the process as circumstances may dictate. There are two distinct neural elements of this control – often working in antagonistic ways. Where one part, the sympathetic system, may up-regulate an activity, usually the parasympathetic system has the opposite effect. It all happens automatically! When we even try to bring some voluntary control to bear on a particular element being run by autonomic control, it is extremely difficult or impossible to override the system, we can barely have even the slightest effect. The system is set up to look after itself – all exquisitely balanced and highly efficient.

When nerve cells develop in fetal life, they all start out in a primitive neural plate that forms from the outer layer of the embryo and gradually folds within the first weeks of development to become the neural tube. It should perhaps not be too surprising that the different elements of the mature nervous system actually come from quite different sources. A population of primitive nerve cells becomes identifiable at the posterior part of the neural plate and becomes known as the neural crest. It is from these cells, that are capable of differentiating into various different mature forms, that components of the autonomic system arise. So, for example, the sympathetic system includes cells in the special chain of aggregated nerve cells called ganglia, which eventually runs in a linked chain all the way from the lower neck to the upper lumbar region of the spine. Some of these cells become specialised and even end up in medulla (the inner section) of the adrenal glands.[15]

A neuroblastoma is a tumour derived from neuroblasts; these are primitive cells of the sympathetic nervous system and while it can affect all ages, it is actually the most common solid tumour in childhood. When it occurs, the specific symptoms depend on where the lesion is. It can arise in the abdomen or chest, but in fact examples can occur wherever these primitive cells can be found, so the possibilities are numerous. The reason that these cells misbehave in this way is not known with any certainty.

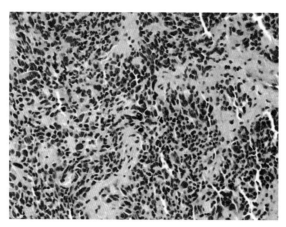

Poorly differentiated neuroblastoma X 400 magnification.

Interestingly, most infants experience complete regression of their disease sometimes with minimal therapy and even with metastatic disease (that is, disease that has spread to other locations thus making treatment much more challenging). When the cases show localised tumours they are almost always curable. By the same token, older patients typically have disease which not only grows relentlessly, they frequently have metastatic deposits where it might have spread to lymph nodes, liver, lung or bone and the unfortunate fact is that the results are awful despite even the most intensive multimodality therapy. Why neuroblastomas show such puzzling characteristics is not really understood.

There remain a whole perplexing set of questions concerning how cancers spread. Is it down to kinetics, metabolism, genetics, epigenetics, and the microenvironment? What gives the metastasising cell its key and distinctive advantage, its mobility and the ability to invade?

For years we have never been terribly sure how to treat early stage invasive breast cancer. Actually, diligent work can shed some useful light on a conundrum like this. It is now possible with some sophisticated genetic work to predict which women with early breast cancer are likely to derive benefit from which treatment option. Breast cancers are usually classified by defining the probable hormone or growth factor sensitivity that the tissue may display, as well as the possible spread of disease to the local lymph nodes. So, for example, tumours may display cell surface receptors for oestrogen, (ER positive or negative) and human epidermal growth factor (HER positive or negative), and these characteristics are considered to be risk markers that relate to the possibility that a patient may develop recurrence of their disease following initial treatment. Each of these characteristics is considered to link to some specific genetic factor in the tumour tissue and it is now possible to use an array of lab tests which measure the activity of multiple genes known to be linked to breast cancer recurrence.

For years the mainstay of breast cancer treatment was surgical excision. By a process of careful analysis and follow up, it has become increasingly clear that surgery ought to play a much less important role in the overall management of this disease. For early tumours, particularly those with the cell surface characteristics that would indicate their likely responsiveness to anti-oestrogen drugs or drugs that can target HER2 status, the most recent debate has been the question of whether these therapies would be enough to really provide the best control or whether additional chemotherapy would also have a role. If only there was a way to answer that particular question.

Using a new multi-gene assay, it is now possible to assign a score that indicates the risk of recurrence. If the score is low – hormone therapy is just fine as an effective treatment. If the recurrence score is high – chemotherapy ought to be added. The problem has been that the vast majority of women, some 70%, fall in a grey zone in the middle where uncertainty reigns as to whether they ought to have chemotherapy or not. The standard approach has been to give the chemotherapy rather than risk failing to offer potentially helpful treatment. Now, on the basis of a study of more than 10,000 women, it is possible to say with some certainty that the group in the middle grey area derive no benefit from adding potentially toxic chemotherapy to their treatment plan. Conundrum solved. Avoid the chemotherapy! Save on toxicity and save the health service a fortune.

Encouragingly, the treatment results now show a chance of survival sitting at a spectacular 98% at 5 years and 94% at 9 years. These results are dramatically better than I was unfortunate enough to witness during my training years in surgical practice. Breast cancer is no longer the threatening and dreaded disease that it used to be.

This kind of massive cooperative research effort has been able to answer an important question. It is reassuring that while the questions multiply at least some answers are being uncovered.

Weird and Wandering

The detective work that often underpins a successful surgical diagnosis can seem like a real puzzle. Following the standard approach with the clinical method and then lining up the most logical investigations in such a way that we get to an answer with the smallest possible number of steps, with the least risk and discomfort to the patient and in the most cost effective way, is usually the nature of the challenge we face. There are few problems in abdominal surgery that really present an enigma. This is not because of the difficulty in reaching an accurate diagnosis but in trying to understand why such a curious phenomenon even exists in the first place.

I recall an 11-year-old girl who presented with recurrent abdominal pain. Her abdominal examination revealed left sided lump. Initially it seemed as though the explanation might be sinister but, in fact, it turned out to be perfectly innocent; it was a wandering spleen. Normally it is not even possible to detect the spleen on clinical examination so when a lump is encountered in the abdomen some distance from where the spleen is almost always located, it is easy to see why there may not be a high index of suspicion that that is what it is. Much more likely that an alternative explanation applies and one can be forgiven for thinking that a most unwelcome diagnosis may be a reasonable conclusion. So, when the true nature of the offending lump was uncovered there was reason for genuine relief all round. At least some surgical conundrums have a straightforward solution. Whip it out! For years, surgeons were rather blasé about the spleen on the basis that people rarely ever miss it. In fact, as the evidence began to accumulate, it became increasingly clear that simply disposing of the spleen was not such a good idea because it opened the door to the possibility of the rapid onset of rare but horrendously aggressive bacterial infections. As far as is possible now, we try to preserve the spleen or at least as much of it as can be saved. Simply to remove it is now considered to be inappropriate treatment for benign splenic conditions. Accordingly, this patient had what might be termed a sub-total splenectomy and she remains healthy and well several years later. But wait; why was the spleen 'wandering' in the first place? This amounts to a true enigma in the surgical world. No one has a foggy notion!

Whether it is headaches, blood pressure, or any member of the curious family of idiopathic or cryptogenic conditions, wandering organs or the challenge of malignant disease in its various forms, we attribute much of our understanding of the cause of disease to basic pathology, physiology, or even basic science. It is virtually always helpful to understand the basis for things.

We like to reduce a problem to the simplest possible explanation. What I suggest to you is this, the more we try to reduce our basic understanding of medicine and biology to the fundamentals of chemistry and physics the more questions, it seems, emerge.

So, what's the answer to that 'wondering' question – do you ever wonder about things? All the time! I have wondered about these things for my entire professional life. In my research I have been able to answer some questions about why cancer cells behave the way they do, what factors may promote or inhibit their growth and why these particular characteristics apply. However, the big fundamental, unanswered questions about such perplexing diseases remain topics about which we can only wonder and try to investigate further. Let's go back to Medawar for a moment. On reflecting about research, he pointed out that coming up with a proposed explanation – a hypothesis – involves an 'imaginative preconception of where the truth might lie.' It would certainly be true to say that we need to keep the informed imagination active. Should we fail to conceive what the solution to a problem might be, the scientific endeavour would grind to a halt.

And the further we go – as I will show you – the more perplexing these questions become.

Take home message ...

Breaking clinical puzzles down to the basic elements of physiology and biochemistry and then, inevitably, to basic chemistry and physics leads to the accumulation of even more layers of perplexing enigmata.

Section 2
Layers of Perplexity

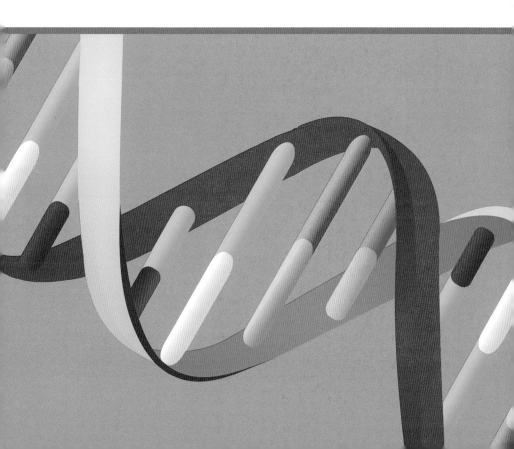

Subtlety and control

Why should things be easy to understand?
Thomas Pynchon [1937-]

ONE OF THE FIRST INTRODUCTIONS I had into clinical research was as a junior member of the academic Department of Surgery in one of Glasgow's premier teaching hospitals. These were the days when research was not quite the big business it seems to have become. Most academics these days are driven along by the need to produce funding for their research ideas and to ensure that they publish their results in a journal with a high impact factor. Things seemed rather gentler 30 years ago and the early forms of this highly professionalised approach to research activity in academic medicine was just picking up speed.

I was invited to join a project examining the role of complement activation in acute pancreatitis. Well for a start, having only recently qualified from medical school, I had seen patients with acute pancreatitis often enough but had only a vague notion of what 'complement' actually was. What a revelation it turned out to be! Within physiology and medicine it is quite possible to become a world authority on some relatively obscure condition or process without trying too hard. There was just such a world authority on complement working in the local pathology department and I rapidly read around the technical literature on this topic. It became clear to me that the medical curriculum was well behind the ball.

Acute pancreatitis can be a very frightening illness. It has a sudden onset and most of the time the likely cause is not immediately clear. It is possible to sort out the aetiology quite quickly in the vast majority of cases and it then becomes a matter of supporting the patient through the acute attack and dealing with the trigger that was responsible for its occurrence in the first place. One of the contributions that came from clinical research in Glasgow resulted from some very perceptive work by a Glasgow surgeon called Clem Imrie.[16] He advanced the idea that with a few carefully chosen blood tests on samples drawn early on in the attack, it was possible to predict how severe the attack would be and provide some insight as to the likely outcome. So-called mild cases settled in a matter of a day or two, but severe acute pancreatitis could not only be complicated and difficult to treat but there can be a significant threat to life. It was very frustrating to see young patients struggle with severe acute pancreatitis and to lose their battle with what amounted to a non-malignant disease. Part of the puzzle was that patients with pancreatitis from identical causes might present with very different disease severity. Why was this the case? We wondered if something was fuelling the fire of the body's response to the attack, resulting in huge over-activity of part of the inflammatory response that in turn resulted in severe local tissue damage and all the resulting sequelae that proved so dangerous to the patient with severe disease.

The complement system is a distinct component of the body's immune system. Its role is to support and amplify the ability of the other elements of the system to do their job efficiently. It is an amazing cascade of some 30 inter-related proteins and enzymes with elaborate control mechanisms, feedback loops, and the ability to ramp up its level of activity very rapidly indeed. It can be set off and running in several different ways. The so-called classical pathway of activation is typically active in tissue that has been damaged or invaded. There is a constant level of low-grade complement activation (known as the alternative pathway) ticking over in the blood stream most of the time ready to charge into full-blown assault should any invading bacterial force mount an attack. Both of these pathways result in activating the complement protein C5, which is composed of two polypeptide chains, linked together. When the enzyme C5 convertase is up-regulated the breakdown products of C5 are independently active – C5a acts as a signalling molecule and is chemotactic, whereas C5b is the first protein in a chain of reactions leading to the assembly of the membrane attack complex.

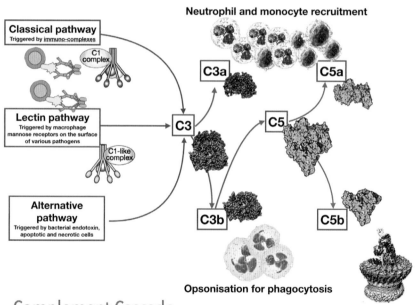

Complement Cascade

Woe betide any bacterium or cell that finds itself in range. It is marked to have a sizeable hole punched in its cell membrane – an assault that would be fatal for that organism. Complement is no respecter of targets. It can sometimes fail to distinguish between the patient's own cells and invading bacteria and so, in a process of immune friendly fire, it can wipe out the body's own tissues in a process that has come to be called bystander lysis. Lysis is the process of cellular destruction by tearing or destroying part of the cell membrane. Once the membrane has been ripped open all the cytoplasmic innards leak out and that cell is dead.

Complement is a powerful inflammatory mediator in the development of a number of autoimmune and inflammatory conditions and our hypothesis was that it might play a part in enhancing the severity of the body's response to acute pancreatitis. Bearing in mind that the pancreas itself is responsible for the secretion of enzymes designed to break up proteins – the digestive proteases perform this function – could it be that some of the protease activity from the host cells of the damaged pancreas was contributing to complement activation and unnecessary acceleration of the inflammatory response, in turn leading to tissue damage which might not have occurred otherwise? Was it responsible for scaling up and amplifying the inflammatory changes such that the outcome behaved like a severe burn at the back of the upper abdominal cavity? Over the years, severe acute pancreatitis has been difficult to treat and it continues to be a significant threat to survival, even now in the 21st Century. We started looking at this carefully and were able to demonstrate complement activation in acute pancreatitis. Thirty years on, the question as to whether such activation is friend or foe in this disease, remains open.[17]

All of this may be fascinating in its own right but there is a more perplexing issue to my mind and it is this: how did this system arise in the first place? When one thinks of the standard mechanism for the development of complexity and diversity in living systems, we are led to consider the possibility that the complexity gradually advanced over a huge time period as a result of genetic copying errors and the filter of natural selection. The concern in my mind is simply this - for that explanation to hold, not only would every gradual improvement in the multiple protein components have to have some selectable advantage but, in addition, the biochemical challenge to forming all these proteins with functional folded shapes and activity appears to face ridiculous probabilistic odds. Is it really possible that a finely-balanced, integrated system, composed of specifically-shaped proteins with feedback loops and sophisticated signalling control could arise in a series of small genetically driven steps (mistakes in DNA copying) such that every such selected step could demonstrate survival advantage to the organism? It seemed preposterous to suggest such a thing. I am not a gambler but I doubt you would find any sane, non-risk averse, gambler who would take on the odds that for this kind of system are unimaginably stacked against the outcome we find. So we are left to advance the question - what was the cause of such a system?

In many respects it shares some of the characteristics of another more familiar system of inter-related proteins. This is another amazing, integrated multi-component group of protease enzymes. These too are organised in a kind of cascade where activation leads to blood coagulation. When a blood vessel is damaged and liquid blood comes spilling out, the machinery spools into action. Successive proteins in the cascade are activated and become adherent to the site of the damage. They funnel towards the production of thrombin from its precursor protein and that thrombin in turn has proteolytic activity on fibrinogen that is converted to fibrin, and in turn the fibrin molecules are hooked together by the formation of crosslinks and so an established and firmer structure is produced as the clot matures. The fibrin lattice is essentially the scaffolding for a new blood clot and tiny cell fragments, the platelets, aggregate amongst the tangle of fibrin fibres resulting in a plug and consequent cessation of leakage from the damaged vessel. All the way along, there are subtle adjustments and enhancements that control the final result and a battery of protein machines are recruited to fashion the end product.

You would be right to suspect that when there are multiple components in such a system, there are numerous opportunities for one or more parts to fail. Either their production is absent or deficient, or controlling or signalling mechanisms falter and can result in malfunction. The malfunction may not rest with the protein coagulation factors; it may be that patients experience a bleeding tendency because their platelets are sparse, or their characteristics are deficient or malfunctioning. Sometimes the problem relates to the effects or side effects of certain drugs. Fortunately, with careful detective work in the laboratory, it is usually possible to identify the problem and either replace the missing component or find a workaround to bring the system back into operation, by bypassing a metabolic blockage and helping to get the machinery downstream in the cascade back into action. Sometimes it is possible for the coagulation pathway to work, at least after a fashion, when there is deficiency of certain links in the cascade. However, when there is a critical step with no easy alternative the lack of ability to form good quality blood clots can be a serious or insurmountable threat to life.

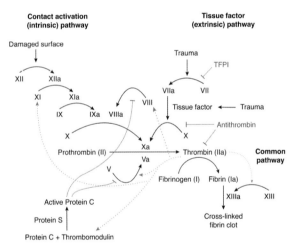

Coagulation Cascade

Such is the machine-like, apparently purposeful, arrangement of all these components that it seems to me inconceivable that the step-by-step gradual mechanism of causation, by a partly random natural process, could deliver not just a complex protein machine but an entire factory of integrated, interconnected, beautifully balanced machines. When the proposed mechanism by which biological systems emerge is utterly dependent on function and therefore selectable advantage, and when the system fails to deliver function if even one component is not present or not working, then such a mechanism clearly cannot explain the end result.

Come to think of it, and as we shall see, there are numerous interrelated nano-machines in virtually every cellular process and where these link together in an integrated system, a system which falters or fails with the critical loss of a single component, the odds against such a system being built step-by-step are so high, the explanation needs to be revised or discarded and a better narrative found. It should now be evident that any complex interlocking biological system cannot be built in a series of small steps which themselves confer no functional advantage. The progressive stages provide no survival advantage and are not therefore selectable. We need a radically different explanation and we'll look at some of the possible alternatives shortly.

I want to return to the wonderful world of micro-molecular machinery later, but for now I would like to examine some examples of large scale (tissue and organ level) systems and some practical implications, rather than the molecular networks we have been focusing on here.

Take home message ...

Biological systems can demonstrate astonishing complexity but the coherence, integration and control makes a step-by-step understanding of causation, untenable. There is evidence of genuine design, and foresight is apparent in virtually every example.

Causation dissected

I HAD NEVER BEEN IN RURAL Africa before. What an assault on the senses and the psyche! I have read and pondered the experiences the great David Livingstone had as he explored that continent. Indeed, I have had the chance to read a first edition copy of his *Missionary Travels and Researches in South Africa*. Livingstone was a quite extraordinary character. From humble beginnings as a 10-year-old worker in the Blantyre Mill, to the south and east of the city of Glasgow, he studied relentlessly to realise his ambition. The mill environment would be intolerable by today's standards: noisy, the air contaminated with cotton dust and the 14-hour shifts started at 6am, Monday through Saturday. A toughening experience if ever there was one. When he was aged 13, he started evening classes to study Latin – 2 hours from 8pm and he would then habitually read and study at home until late at night. He consumed books of many different kinds. Apparently he was no great enthusiast for novels or theological books but rather travel or science; these were the topics that were of much greater interest. His work in those days was driven by his desire to study at the Medical School of Anderson's University in Glasgow. He worked for years to save enough to afford the £12 annual college fees and he started his course in 1836 and completed it with the award of his degree from the Faculty of Physicians and Surgeons of Glasgow in 1840. He was an outstanding student and hesitatingly decided to enrol with the London Missionary Society and as a result gained some financial help to complete his studies.

David Livingstone [1813-1873] by Thomas Annan.
Medical missionary and explorer.

His degree certificate is displayed on the wall of the Livingstone Room in what has become the Royal College of Physicians and Surgeons of Glasgow. Despite the prospect of a secure teaching position at the University, his initial plan was to travel to China as a medical missionary. This ambition began to waver, however, and when the First Opium War started in 1840 he decided instead to head for Africa. His place in history is that of legend. He became known as the fearless and dogged explorer, helping both medically and, where he could, by advancing the Christian gospel. He was keen to promote trade, to bring an end to slavery and in the process he became the first European to navigate his way across Africa.

By all accounts Livingstone wasn't the easiest person to work with and had many a spat with colleagues from Great Britain. His personal friendships with the Africans were more surefooted and convivial. From the banks of the Clyde to the banks of the Zambezi – so it was that I followed at least part of Livingstone's route to that mighty African river.

My route to Chitokoloki in the North Western province of rural Zambia was a good deal more straightforward and dramatically faster that Livingstone's 19th century exploits. I flew in to Lusaka for the first time in September 2015 and from there met Canadian mission pilot Chris Brundage who flew me onwards in a Cessna 206 to the Zambian bush – a three-hour flight, cruising at 10,000 feet, north and west to Chitokoloki International Airport. Actually in reality there is no airport. There is a clearing with a dirt airstrip and after an initial pass to check the state of the windsock and to ensure that there were no goats or people on the runway we came in to a smooth landing and a clattering taxi to the hangar where the plane was parked and tied down for the night.

I have written elsewhere[18] about my experience as a visiting surgeon in a rural African mission hospital but it was there that I was reintroduced to the marvel of the hypothalamo-pituitary axis.

Now, I am no endocrinologist, although I may once have described myself as a metabolic surgeon! That involved treating patients with severe obesity and type II diabetes by means of advanced laparoscopic (or keyhole) surgical techniques. The vast majority of Western patients who are diabetic are also markedly obese – obesity is not at all common in rural Africa; quite the opposite. With a background in General Surgery, I volunteered to help Dr. David McAdam, a surgeon who hails originally from Northern Ireland and who has spent his entire career as a missionary doctor in central Africa, both Congo and rural Zambia. David provided me with an introduction to missionary medical and surgical practice. The hospital is small – 4 wards, male and female general wards, a maternity ward, and a paediatric ward. There are two well-equipped operating theatres, both air conditioned, so that in itself was a significant incentive to spend time there! The breadth of practice David McAdam is able to offer in Chitokoloki is truly amazing. There is no supporting specialist hospital so almost all the specialties are served single-handedly by the in-house team of a couple of doctors and a group of nurses and midwives. It was an interesting transition to move from a highly specialist practice in a teaching hospital setting in Glasgow, where my practice had progressively been more and more specialised, to Africa where there were no urologists, gynaecologists, orthopaedic or plastic surgeons, no vascular specialists, neither paediatric surgeons nor neurosurgeons and certainly no maxillo-facial surgeons. So I had to call on all my training in some of these disciplines from years before and actually it was amazing to realise just what can be done safely and to a high standard with the application of surgical first principles and good internet connection!

Even more interesting, there were no anaesthetists. Now for surgeons, and I do admit that while we have a tendency to take the skills of our colleagues in anaesthesia for granted, it is quite difficult to operate on someone who is uncooperative, wriggling around and not adequately sedated or anaesthetised. Far better to have the patient pain-free by means of local or regional anaesthesia and for major invasive cases, completely under general anaesthetic. A very experienced midwife, called Julie Rachel Elwood, expertly provided general anaesthesia in Chitokoloki. She functioned not only as the consultant anaesthetist, but was also the obstetrician, surgical registrar, theatre manager, and a host of other roles – quite an astonishing skill set!

So many of the cases in Africa were memorable, some because they were tragic and locally untreatable, although they could have been readily managed in the West. Some, because of the advanced nature of the pathology on presentation, actually so much so, that it made me re-evaluate the advanced pathology that, until that point, I have really only seen in surgical textbooks showing gross examples of various diseases. In Africa the examples are dramatically more memorable, more advanced and more challenging. It makes the textbook cases look a bit pathetic in comparison.

The other major distinction is just how tough these African patients are. In the West, postoperative patients are typically treated with heavy-duty pain controlling drugs in the immediate postoperative period. In rural Zambia there were no opiates available, so these stoic patients made do with a couple of days' treatment with simple paracetamol as their pain control. They just accept the situation – actually they don't really have much choice.

As I spent some time there, the one area with which I felt least comfortable was dealing with the obstetric cases. Mercifully there are wonderful and experienced nurses who are well trained, highly experienced and expert in coping in that resource-limited environment. However, there was always the threat of an emergency Caesarian section and while simple cases do not, as a rule, present any major challenge, some obstetric emergencies can be dramatic and threaten two lives and not just one.

It was just such an obstetric emergency that brought back the unexpected link between babies in the bush and the pituitary. Let me unfold the background and the story.

In my career I can safely say that I have rarely lost a patient as a result of uncontrollable bleeding. Catastrophic blood loss can occur and patients who die as a result of massive haemorrhage are usually memorable. Very early in my career there was an incident when a teacher from a local secondary school was admitted via the major resuscitation area in the hospital. He had multiple injuries with significant chest and pelvic trauma. In his acute distress I can remember trying to reassure him without really appreciating the gravity of his situation. Everything that could be done for him was done but despite our best efforts he died shortly after admission from his injuries and there is no doubt that profound blood loss was a contributing factor. It is excessively rare to run into uncontrollable bleeding in an elective surgical procedure. However, it does happen and I well remember such a patient. She was the mother of a clergyman and over many months I had got to know the family of this particular lady very well. As her ovarian cancer progressed, she was treated aggressively with chemotherapy but unfortunately having had several abdominal operations in the past she presented with acute intestinal obstruction. At the time of surgery she had deposits of disease scattered throughout her peritoneal (abdominal) cavity and it soon became obvious that she was not forming blood clots efficiently at all. During a major operation, the occurrence of coagulopathy or a failure of blood coagulation can be a huge problem. We rapidly enlisted the help of colleagues in haematology and it was such a shame that she had an unsuspected problem with what is known as a para-neoplastic syndrome and her widespread ovarian tumour was linked to this desperate and ultimately fatal complication; disseminated intravascular coagulation. In essence, all the protein coagulation factors normally present in the blood stream are inappropriately used up, thus when the demand is made for the coagulation cascade to swing into action, it proves to be inefficient even when aggressive attempts are made to replace the proteins by means of infusion – typically it is difficult to keep pace and on this occasion my patient succumbed.

Massive blood loss is a significant threat whenever it occurs, but surgical or obstetric haemorrhage in rural, resource-poor Zambia is even more of a challenge. That coupled with the fact that the average level of circulating haemoglobin in the rural African population amounts to about half the level expected in UK patients as a result of the other chronic illnesses that diminish the blood count. These include poor nutrition, bilharzia or schistosomiasis with its accompanying splenic enlargement and portal hypertension all contribute. Malaria is an additional, ever present threat. It is not unusual to encounter patients in Africa who appear to function reasonably well, actually, surprisingly well, with a circulating haemoglobin concentration of

60-70 g/L. The range that guides most doctors to regard a result as 'normal' is 120-160g/L – a little higher in men than in women. It is astonishing that African patients have the capacity to get around and fulfil their daily activities having compensated physiologically to cope with such a low oxygen-carrying capacity in their blood. When a patient experiences rapid blood loss from whatever cause, it is vitally important to restore both the circulating blood volume as well as restoring the oxygen-carrying capability of the blood. Blood is the best replacement and providing a safe transfusion requires careful cross matching of the donor blood with the patient's blood in order to avoid a catastrophic transfusion reaction, which itself can threaten the patient's life. On the occasion of the immune system encountering an antigen or molecular characteristic (perhaps a protein or protein-carbohydrate complex) that is not present on the individual's own cells, it will prepare an attack against that antigen and in so doing will destroy the cells bearing that particular target.

The transfusion laboratory, therefore, will take time to perform a match which takes account of the major cell surface characteristics (antigens) of the blood cells which, if not compatible between donor and recipient, would provoke a dramatic immune response. The antigen markers concerned are known as A and B. So an individual may have blood cells with one or the other of these, or both, thus A, B or AB. Where neither are present, they would be classified as blood group O. Normally, each individual has antibodies specifically targeted against the A and B antigens which are not present on their own red cells. Typically, even with massive blood loss, it is usually possible to use various types of fluid to support the circulation until safe, fully cross-matched blood is available. In critical circumstances where life is in danger as a result of blood loss, there is a need for immediate transfusion and it is necessary to give un-cross-matched blood. Such are the characteristics of blood cells that we know it is almost always safe to provide un-cross-matched blood which is Group O and free from other known reactive antigens such as the Rhesus antigen. The ABO and Rhesus systems are the principal antigens although there are many more which can cause trouble from time to time. When there is a need for massive blood transfusion, it is important to consider all the components of lost circulating fluid – not just haemoglobin but also platelets, coagulation factors, and certain salts. It is also sometimes useful to use drugs to modify elements of the coagulation cascade. Accuracy in all of these manoeuvres is based on regular and detailed contact with the laboratory and in sophisticated healthcare systems it is usually possible to deal with the threat of massive blood loss rapidly and efficiently.

Massive bleeding in parts of rural Africa is a completely different ball game. In places like Chitokoloki (which is relatively well equipped) it is possible to carry out basic blood cross matching but the more esoteric tests would be beyond the scope of the laboratory. Of more profound importance, the sad reality is that despite having a national blood transfusion service, the actual supplies of blood for transfusion remain woefully short of the demand. During one of my visits to the African bush, the arrival of the mission plane was eagerly awaited because it was carrying blood for the blood bank. My heart sank when I saw the provision – four units of packed red blood cells; for a whole month! That supply could have been exhausted for a single patient in the space of an hour! It is not hard to see that the consequences of haemorrhage in a resource-poor setting are very different when compared to that with which most Western patients are familiar.

It was just such an emergency involving a Zambian girl that stands out in my mind. It was memorable not just because she came perilously close to losing her life as a result of haemorrhage, but having overcome that acute problem a new, and for me, unexpected development then emerged. Having made a good recovery from her profound obstetric bleed this young mother developed Sheehan's syndrome. During the time that her circulation was threatened by the huge loss of circulating blood volume, the oxygen delivery to various organs and tissues was likely to be seriously compromised.

When the kidneys are affected, acute renal failure can ensue. There are different consequences for other vital organs such as the heart, the lungs and, of course, the brain. A loss of blood can result in a dangerous drop in blood pressure resulting in failure of perfusion of blood to the active and essential target organs. In Sheehan's syndrome the important pituitary gland, located in the base of the brain, is damaged. It has a high metabolic demand and is extremely sensitive to oxygen deprivation.

In normal circumstances the pituitary and the adjacent and related region of the brain known as the hypothalamus work together to regulate and control a myriad of chemical messenger functions, which are actuated through several different endocrine organs which themselves have an array of different effects. These include the thyroid, the parathyroids, the breasts, the adrenals, the gonads, and the skin and through these organs there are multiple additional effects. When the pituitary is damaged by an obstetric or post-partum bleed, one common outcome is that the production of prolactin fails and the patient is unable to produce breast milk to feed her new baby. Around half of the patients will end up with multiple hormone deficiencies because of the secondary effects of losing pituitary function – in other cases perhaps just one or two hormone deficiencies will be noted.

In the UK or USA, a readily available solution for agalactorrhea can be rapidly found. A quick trip to the pharmacy or supermarket and one can be kitted out with milk formula to replace breast milk, together with the necessary bottles, sterilising tablets, and all the paraphernalia that goes along with infant feeding. That solution is not a likely option in the African bush. The sub-Saharan solution is not to nip down to a local specialist supplier, but the surprising and wonderfully effective solution was to buy the family a goat. Goat's milk - job done!

Hold on a second – it surely begs the question; how can dropping your blood pressure and potentially knocking off a few cells in a tiny pea-sized structure on the under surface of the brain have the effect of stopping lactation and, sometimes, for that matter, shutting down the thyroid, parathyroids, adrenals, and so on? Well, the fact is, that the tiny pituitary controls the whole deal.

What an astonishing system - amazingly integrated. Incredibly nuanced control, actually layers of control - even the controlling hormones are themselves controlled. There are negative feedback loops buffering the production of chemical messengers. There are even positive feedback loops, serving to amplify the changes as they occur, for example, in stimulating and accentuating uterine contractions during labour.

The hypothalamus is the command and control centre for the endocrine or hormone system of the body. In essence, it is responsible for monitoring and activating the chemical responses made by the various endocrine organs, like the thyroid, adrenals, and gonads, to various changes which may occur to the body's internal environment, as well as coordinating the way our physiology reacts to changing external circumstances such as the light-dark cycle, temperature change, and stress of various types. It has a direct influence on mental activity, the immune response, digestion, fluid management, metabolism, and energy storage or mobilisation. It also has an effect on sexual function. As an example of how the specific integration works it is worth considering the so-called hypothalamo – pituitary – adrenal axis.

Specialised neurons in the central region of the hypothalamus produce two peptides; vasopressin and corticotrophin-releasing hormone. These are carried in a low pressure system of blood vessels and activate cells in the anterior portion of the pituitary stimulating them to produce a polypeptide hormone called ACTH (adreno-cortico-trophic-hormone) which, in turn, switches on the production of cortisol, the main steroid hormone produced by the outer layer of the adrenal glands. Many cells have the ability to respond to cortisol because they have surface receptors providing

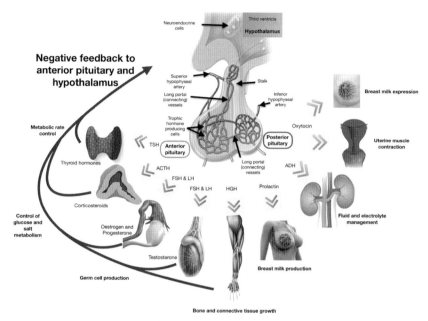

Hypothalamo-pituitary axis

that sensitivity. It has a huge variety of effects on different target tissues. It is sometimes known as the main stress hormone and it helps to maintain the correct working conditions for body physiology to function efficiently in whatever circumstances exist. It helps to control blood sugar levels, blood pressure by influencing salt and water metabolism, and body temperature by influencing blood vessels and sweat glands in the skin. When levels of cortisol are too high there are various adverse effects on mental health, cardiovascular health, weight, connective tissue and bone density. The hypothalamus, in turn, is sensitive to blood levels of cortisol and its production can be down-regulated by reducing the production of corticotrophin releasing hormone when the prevailing cortisol levels exceed demand. This arrangement is known as a negative feedback system. The arrangement of other systemic axes involving the pituitary include the hypothalamo – pituitary – thyroid axis and the hypothalamo – pituitary – gonadal axis are similar with the relevant corresponding negative feedback loops.

117

We saw earlier how complex integrated systems involving the activity of specific proteins can work together to stop bleeding and fight infection. This is now an example of similar subtle levels of signalling and control, actually layers of control at the level of endocrine organs and tissues. Here, astonishingly, there are chemically sensitive tissues that react by producing a chain reaction of additional chemicals which themselves serve to signal to their target cells, in turn, provoking release of their products which themselves trigger the secretion of the hormones typically serving to modulate the initial chemical signal. Intuitively, we see a system with all its component parts functioning in such an efficient and integrated way and we should be forgiven for marvelling at the exquisite design. It certainly meets the criteria of any designed system where there is the purposeful arrangement of parts. The obvious conclusion is that such a system must have been conceived and designed. Not so fast – a famous (and sometimes divisive) science writer is often quoted for his description of biological systems, 'Biology is the study of complicated things that give the appearance of having been designed for a purpose.'[19] Indeed they do. So what do we make of this – is the design real or is it an illusion? Good question. Whatever we make of it we face the same problem that I highlighted earlier. This is analogous to the complex inter-related proteins and enzymes in the coagulation and the complement systems and like those systems, this is another refined, balanced, interlocking biological system which could not be built in a series of small steps. Each step would have to have a demonstrable functional advantage affecting the survival of the organism to have any prospect of becoming selected and genetically fixed in the population. Building a nuanced system like the hypothalamo-pituitary axis demands a different mechanism. There are such mechanisms under active study and I want to look at these shortly. However before we do, let me take one more almost unbelievable example – not from proteins, or endocrine tissues but, this time, from body structure and its related function.

When I first encountered this example, it stopped me in my intellectual tracks. This concerns one of the most stressful events in anyone's life. Dramatic changes are required and there are only seconds to spare or life changing, perhaps even life threatening, consequences apply. It is maybe just as well that we not only must have successfully negotiated this particular challenge to be able to read this account, but also, it is perhaps a mercy that we do not have any recollection of the experience we all have had. I am referring to the incredible events that apply as a baby gets to the end of the birth canal during delivery. For those born by what is sometimes called an operative delivery the same challenges arise. Let's have a look.

It cannot have escaped your notice that the method by which an unborn baby has its oxygen needs met is very different from that for the baby immediately after birth. The changes that take place in the baby's heart and lungs are awe-inspiring and they have to work efficiently and quickly to avoid a tragic outcome. To set the background, allow me to describe and compare the fetal and infant circulation and then we can better appreciate what has to happen to move from the delivery of oxygen via the placenta and the maternal circulation to an independent system where the delivery of oxygen is handled by the lungs. Massive changes are required. They need to be timed to perfection, coordinated, and accurate for a satisfactory outcome.

There are several important differences between the fetus and the newborn baby. First of all, even the structure of haemoglobin, the oxygen carrying protein in the blood, is different and is specialised according to the prevailing conditions. As we will see, in the fetus there is a mixture of oxygen-rich blood with less well oxygenated blood that does not occur in the normal mature circulation. This results in a relatively low partial pressure of O_2.

In order to compensate for this, the baby's haemoglobin must be able to bind oxygen with greater affinity. To accomplish this, its structure comprises four protein subunits rather than two and these react very differently to other compounds that influence oxygen binding. The most dramatic changes, however, take place in the way the blood circulation is organised and in the site of gas exchange.

In the infant (and for that matter the adult) the blood follows a circuitous but predictable and straightforward pathway. From the powerful left ventricle of the heart – its most powerful pumping chamber, blood is ejected at high speed and sufficient pressure to course through the arterial system, delivering oxygen and nutrients to every organ, tissue, and cell in the body. As it moves through

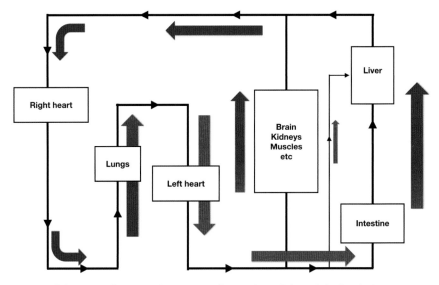

Schematic diagram showing configuration of the adult circulation
(Red indicates fully oxygenated blood and blue, deoxygenated blood)

the smaller and smaller vessels, it finally reaches the network of capillaries, offloads its oxygen before returning towards the right side of the heart by an ever-enlarging network of veins until it finally reaches the vena cava (from the Latin – 'hollow veins') and flows into the right atrium. From here it passes through a valve into the right ventricle before being squeezed out into the pulmonary arteries, sent round the pulmonary circuit where in close proximity to the tiny air sacs known as alveoli the deoxygenated haemoglobin becomes oxygenated once more. It then flows on to the left atrium of the heart before being transferred to the left ventricle once again to complete the process over and over again.

In the fetus, because the lungs are not active in oxygen provision and, indeed, they are both collapsed and filled with fluid, the blood picks up its oxygen by coming into extremely close contact with the oxygen-rich blood in the maternal circulation in the placenta. This fetal stream which leaves the placenta, having been enriched with oxygen, is then presented to the heart for pumping from an entirely different direction and source as compared to the situation following birth, where the oxygenated blood comes from the pulmonary circuit. It is immediately evident that there needs to be an entirely different arrangement for the fetal circulation to function. The necessary objective, of course, is the same, to ensure adequate blood supply to the baby's organs and systems and this therefore involves re-routing the circulation through several so-called shunts or bypass channels. There are three important shunts.

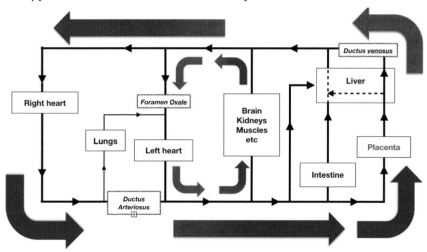

Schematic diagram showing configuration of the fetal circulation

If we consider the fetal circulation from the same starting point as the adult circulation, blood leaves the left ventricle and shoots off round the rest of the circulation in a similar way to the arrangement in the adult. This ensures that the demanding organs like the brain and kidneys have their oxygen demands met. The arterial tree in the fetus has an additional route to the placenta through the two

121

umbilical arteries. Bear in mind that, in contrast to the mature circulation where the arterial blood is rich in oxygen, the fetal arterial tree contains blood that needs to be enriched with oxygen.

It achieves this by being distributed in a network of vessels of ever-decreasing diameter until it is brought into close proximity with the maternal blood. There is no physical contact or mixing of the two circulations between mother and baby. The newly oxygenated blood is then returned to the baby's circulation by means of the umbilical vein which heads for the fetal liver.

Approximately half of the oxygenated umbilical venous blood is distributed to the liver; the remainder bypasses the liver through the first important shunt, the so-called ductus venosus. In essence, this provides for a supply of oxygen-rich blood to be available to the other important organs. The blood supply to the liver is rather complicated but for our purposes the shunted blood in the ductus venosus is bound for the main venous channel from the lower half of the body, the inferior vena cava. This oxygen-rich blood drains into the inferior vena cava (IVC) through a common channel with the left hepatic vein. The latter contains blood from which much of the oxygen has been extracted thus there is a risk that the oxygen levels in the resulting stream are further compromised. Spare a thought for the brain, kidney and heart muscle cells waiting patiently for their much-needed oxygen to arrive. This is where an amazing and subtle design feature comes into play as the respective streams of blood head for the right side of the heart. The configuration of the vessels here maintains a degree of separation between the oxygen rich blood and the blood that has already offloaded its oxygen in the tissues through which it has passed.

All the blood that leaves the liver, either through the *left* hepatic vein or the ductus venosus, leaves through a single orifice. Astonishingly, and this is clever, the well oxygenated blood selectively streams in the posterior and left portion of the *inferior* vena cava, heading in the direction of the foramen ovale, allowing it to bypass the right side of the heart and enter the left atrium. The less well oxygenated blood from the *right* hepatic vein joins blood returning from the distal inferior vena cava streaming along the anterior and right portions of the inferior vena cava and selectively streams towards the tricuspid valve to enter the right ventricle. So the oxygen-rich blood from the placenta that emerges from the ductus venosus not only maintains a measure of distinction from the rest of the hepatic and vena caval flow, it is selectively directed through that vitally important shunt – a hole between the right and left atria within the heart itself, the foramen ovale, thus allowing the majority of this blood to bypass the pulmonary circuit. There would be no point in sending a load of blood round the rudimentary lungs anyway – there is no oxygen to collect there and the vessels are closed down and can only tolerate a tiny volume compared with what happens when they expand after birth. The ductus arteriosus allows the major share of the cardiac output from the right side of the heart to bypass the

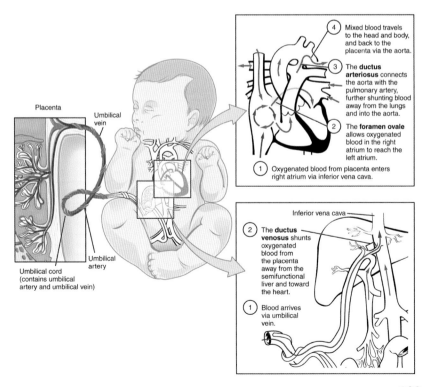

Placenta

Umbilical vein

Umbilical cord (contains umbilical artery and umbilical vein)

Umbilical artery

4 Mixed blood travels to the head and body, and back to the placenta via the aorta.

3 The **ductus arteriosus** connects the aorta with the pulmonary artery, further shunting blood away from the lungs and into the aorta.

2 The **foramen ovale** allows oxygenated blood in the right atrium to reach the left atrium.

1 Oxygenated blood from placenta enters right atrium via inferior vena cava.

Inferior vena cava

2 The **ductus venosus** shunts oxygenated blood from the placenta away from the semifunctional liver and toward the heart.

1 Blood arrives via umbilical vein.

pulmonary circulation and get on with the business of delivering oxygen to the systemic circulation. All of this sophistication has been demonstrated and confirmed using Doppler colour flow techniques in the human fetus – the flow from the ductus venosus can be seen streaming directly through the inferior vena cava, through the foramen ovale and into the left atrium.[20]

The reason that the right to left shunt, the foramen ovale, is so important is that it selectively allows the stream that has come from the placenta via the ductus venosus to deliver its precious oxygen cargo to the tissues that need it most without diluting it by admixing deoxygenated blood from other tissues and organs.

Interestingly, and by this time you should not be surprised to learn that the blood returning from the brain and upper torso via the *superior* vena cava (SVC) also appears to undergo a selective streaming effect. This occurs, courtesy of a very subtle prominence just above the fossa ovalis, the so-called tubercle of Lower or intervenous tubercle, thus directing the stream of deoxygenated blood away from the oxygen-rich placental blood as it heads for the foramen ovale. So in fact, there is a system of dual preferential streaming, (from the IVC to the patent foramen ovale and from the SVC to the atrio-ventricular (tricuspid) valve). This effect, which was initially suspected and recognised back in the 1930s[21] has been more recently accurately mapped by magnetic resonance velocity studies.[22] The SVC stream is seen to flow over the convex muscular surface of the anterior right atrial wall and is directed towards the atrio-ventricular valve.

This kind of streaming effect is sometimes named after the Romanian aerodynamics engineer who first described it in 1910 – Henri Marie Coanda.[23] Both of these preferential streams are important and inter-related. Malfunction in one could interfere with flow in the other thus disturbing the function of the right to left shunt through the foramen ovale. The contours of the atrial walls, therefore, appear to contribute to this Coanda effect, keeping the two streams of blood apart and allowing optimal oxygen delivery within the fetal circulation.

That sounds pretty impressive, but the changes that all have to occur at birth, starting within the first few seconds, are utterly mind boggling.

I don't know whether you have ever delivered a baby. It is a slightly weird, exciting, and strangely exhilarating experience. Labour – and, as a man, I hesitate to even mention the word – appears to be exactly as named. It can be a long, maybe very long, and painful struggle. Recalling our earlier visit to the hypothalamo – pituitary axis, you will remember that it is involved in this process by the secretion of oxytocin, which, in the control of the early and active aspects of the first stage of labour, drives the rhythmic uterine contractions to begin, build up and with the dilatation of the cervix, prepares the way for the drama of the second stage to begin. I guess, if you are an obstetrician, even the action of the second stage, when the baby is actually delivered through the birth canal, is not really much of a drama but for most of us lesser mortals, it is one of the most awe inspiring and memorable moments we ever encounter. I remember being guided through this process as a medical student and in professional life did not encounter labour again until I was working in rural Africa. Mercifully, I was protected from most of the gory details but did, on many occasions, have to become involved surgically when it became obvious that, as a result of failure of the process to progress or because of fetal distress, a surgical delivery was the only solution. Whether by the natural route or by Caesarian section, when the baby is born, everything suddenly changes – and all of a sudden, he or she is required to breathe air. This is all a huge shock to the system, of course, and while we focus on and listen for, that first hearty cry, some even more astonishing changes need to take place and to take place quickly.

As the baby is delivered from the safety and warmth of the uterus, clamps are typically placed on the umbilical cord and right away the source of oxygen is cut off. Even without the clamps the placenta will be delivered and will have served its purpose. So the baby needs oxygen and fast. It is amazing how quickly the newborn, deprived of oxygen, turns a dusky, inky blue colour, this being the effect of stripping all the oxygen from the baby's haemoglobin as it is used up in the tissues.

So, not only is there a sudden requirement for life-giving oxygen, there are huge changes going on in the circulation. The flow of blood in the umbilical vein is instantly switched off. Given that around 40% of the combined cardiac output is directed via the umbilical vessels, turning this off requires rapid adaptation and adjustments to be made.

As the first breath is taken and that welcome yell pierces the air, the lungs expand enormously and the fluid-filled spaces now become a spongy network of millions of air-filled alveoli. An additional effect of lung expansion is the sudden drop in the blood pressure within the pulmonary vessels, allowing a dramatic increase in flow, to meet the needs of the newly minted gas exchange system that, with every breath, is now operational.

Because of the changes in the routing of the circulating blood from a complicated fetal, parallel arrangement with several shunts and connecting channels, these are all progressively closed – a process that begins immediately and normally takes around 7 to 10 days to be completed.

All of these changes take place in a blur, triggered by switching from intra to extra uterine life – it begs several questions. How do all these changes happen and given that all these systemic alterations need to take place together and in a balanced controlled and coordinated way, how on earth did such a system develop in the first place? Let me tackle these issues in turn.

First, what are the physiological drivers that allow such biological integration to work?

It turns out that there is a combination of physical and chemical factors at play in delivering and coordinating all the necessary changes. Let's consider it as a series of distinct events, even although we bear in mind that they are inter-related and simultaneous.

When the cord is clamped and the umbilical blood flow drops to zero there is a significant fall in the volume of blood returning to the heart via the ductus venosus and inferior vena cava. This leads

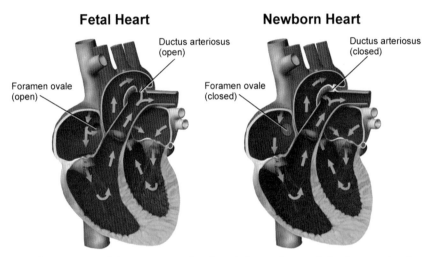

Fetal Heart

Ductus arteriosus
(open)

Foramen ovale
(open)

Newborn Heart

Ductus arteriosus
(closed)

Foramen ovale
(closed)

to a lowering of the pressure in the right atrium of the heart. At the same time the lungs inflate with air and steady ventilation starts – as it does, there is a marked expansion in the pulmonary vascular volume and a significant reduction in the resistance to flow within these vessels as they open up. Part of the muscular wall of the tiny lung vessels is very reactive to levels of oxygen in the circulation and as the hypoxic conditions change to oxygen-rich conditions, the vessels dilate up and flow increases. In addition, it is thought that chemical factors within the endothelial cells lining these small arteries, together with nitric oxide, play a part in adjusting the pulmonary circulation. As the flow increases, the pressure in the left atrium also increases. Because of the flap valve nature of the foramen ovale, it closes mainly because of these pressure changes

127

on each side of the divide and the apposed leaflets then gradually fuse creating a seal.

Over the ensuing few weeks, the now redundant and occluded ductus venosus is steadily replaced with fibrous connective tissue and is designated the 'ligamentum venosum.'

The remaining right to left shunt is the ductus arteriosus. Like the other two, it becomes superfluous to requirements in the neonatal circulation. While it does not physically close for a few days, the flow through this shunt from the pulmonary trunk to the aorta is almost completely eliminated. The current understanding of the trigger to the closure of this arterial shunt relies on the oxygen-sensitive smooth muscle cells in the wall of the ductus, such that lung ventilation leading to an increase in the prevailing oxygen tension, together with a fall in the plasma levels of prostaglandin E2 activate these concentrically arranged muscle cells. As a result, the channel narrows down and finally closes completely, eventually becoming replaced by fibrous tissue.

Beyond the amazing physiology, we come to a second conundrum. Clearly a system like this has to work straight out of the blocks. If any significant component failed for whatever reason, anatomical anomaly, biochemical error or signalling failure, not only would the various changes be jeopardised, but the very survival of the newly-born infant would be seriously threatened. The amazing truth is that thousands of babies navigate this dangerous territory, every minute of every day. So, given our current understanding of the origin of complex systems in biology, how might such an exquisite arrangement have developed?

It looks like an analogous conundrum to the development of some of the other integrated systems we have considered. To claim that they could be built, step by gradual step is beginning to seem like a common concern for such systems. Those who assert that such a mechanism is responsible have an insurmountable burden of proof to sustain that position. Whatever the mechanism, it is evident that a gradual process, such as underpins the generally accepted paradigm for the development of complicated biological systems, is clearly not a mechanism that would work. We need a totally different understanding – we'll look at the possibilities soon but there are more questions to consider first.

These are just a few physiological examples of enormously complex, exquisitely controlled, amazingly effective, and specified systems bearing all the hall marks of design and for which there is no satisfactory adequate developmental mechanism to which we can appeal for an explanation.

Does that mean that we are unable to infer any adequate explanation? I suspect not, but before I assemble that case there are even more astonishing elements in the story that deserve to be explored. This is where the narrative becomes more perplexing still. The nanotech within the cell provides similar examples of systems and machines that appear to defy explanation. Let's take a look.

Take home message ...

The more detailed the examination of physiological systems the more amazing are the hierarchies of modulation and control. To assume that such systematic structural and functional organisation emerged as a result of unguided natural processes stretches beyond the limits of credulity.

Complexity and Causation.
Nano tech in subcellular life

To grasp the reality of life as it has been revealed by molecular biology, we must magnify a cell a thousand million times until it is twenty kilometers in diameter and resembles a giant airship large enough to cover a great city like London or New York. What we would then see would be an object of unparalleled complexity and adaptive design. On the surface of the cell we would see millions of openings, like the port holes of a vast space ship, opening and closing to allow a continual stream of materials to flow in and out. If we were to enter one of these openings we would find ourselves in a world of supreme technology and bewildering complexity.

Michael Denton [1943-]

WE ARE MADE OF AMAZING stuff. Think of the variety, a skeleton made from complex combinations of the proteins, collagen and inorganic calcium, soft tissues of a huge variety, each with a specific signature of constituents including proteins, carbohydrates, and fats. Some proteins, like the scaffolding found in bone and connective tissue, are principally structural but many proteins are machines. Some have suggested that referring to them in this way is just a linguistic trick. In fact, the claim goes, the notion of a protein machine is really just analogical. Maybe proteins can show some machine-like characteristics but to call them machines is surely a bit of a stretch. It may be convenient in helping us describe what they do but it is hardly a reflection of reality. Is that a fair assessment? Are these so-called molecular machines really machine-like but perhaps not actual machines in the sense that we would normally recognise? This is not an entirely trivial issue. To address it we might first ask how we could best express the definition of a machine? Well, it is a little tricky to come up with an all-encompassing defining phrase but there are certainly several identifiable elements which are common to machines of whatever size, shape or function so, how about this? A 'machine is a piece of apparatus, often composed of several components, which uses an energy source to perform a particular physical effect or accomplish a specific task.' Of course, they come in all sorts of varieties and the way in which they go about their business can appear to be quite imaginative. It is interesting to see how different types of energy can be redirected to perform the function for which an individual machine appears to be designed. Some channel electrical energy, others manipulate chemical reactions or perhaps harness or redirect gravitational or magnetic force for a specific reason. Virtually every man-made machine we encounter fails to capitalise on all the energy with which it is presented. Some are more efficient than others, but it is very unusual to come across a machine that can be considered to be even close to ideal; that is, a machine with a power output that is equal to the power input. Inevitably, movement is involved and so friction has to be overcome, indeed the more complex a machine, the more moving parts it is likely to have and, therefore, the more inefficient it is likely to be.

Most of the machines we encounter are woefully inefficient. Take a car with an internal combustion engine; our best estimates are that it is about 30% efficient in terms of turning the energy stored in the fuel into kinetic energy and moving the car from A to B. In comparison, steam turbines are usually better, at 50-60%, whereas a good quality electric motor can produce efficiency performance figures in the region of 90% or more.

Some machines we use regularly can be very efficient. Extraordinary claims are made in support of the humble bicycle as delivering work output that is a better match for the effort put in to turning the pedals. Even here, there is considerable energy loss through the chain, bearings, gears, and even the need to overcome wind and road surface resistance.

By far the most efficient machines we know are the amazing molecular machines within each living cell. There is no doubt that they would satisfy the demands of our definition and therefore are genuine machines. It is hard to know exactly how many different protein machines our cells contain. A conservative estimate would be somewhere between tens of thousands to hundreds of thousands

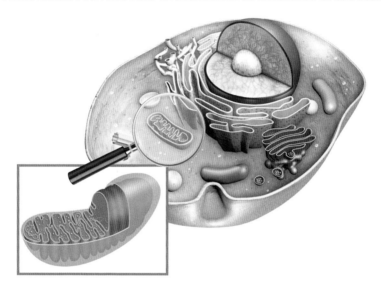

Diagram of a mammalian cell showing the double membrane bound organelle (mitochondrion) in the inset.

per cell; just to keep the cells alive, respiring, metabolising, moving, reproducing, and doing all the different things they do both in us and for us. Some of our intracellular molecular machines spin, others crawl or pump, grab or even eject or inject. Some load and unload cargo. Some are involved in packaging. Some are motors, others are generators. There are switches, assemblers, gates, clamps, turbines, ratchets, and winding machines. Cellular metabolism and function is a veritable factory populated by automatic, specific, exquisitely balanced, super efficient, manufactured machines. The key features of each machine include its physical size and shape, but also the specific reactive molecules or arrangements of molecules within the structure that are crucial to what it actually does. We'll look at a few examples in a moment. It is surely worth asking whether this world of microscopic machinery, which is running the show in every living cell, emerged as a result of some un-designed set of coincidental chemical reactions, assisted by time and some selective influence or filter. Or, as may seem more intuitive, were they in some way designed by a process or mechanism as yet unknown? I cannot think of any machine with an arrangement of components assembled in such a way as to produce a particular function that has not been conceived, designed and built for that purpose. And, I suggest, neither can you! So, we have an enigma. I am too much of a skeptic to swallow the story that complex protein machines just happened!

It will suffice for me to give examples of some of the more awesome molecular machines I have come across. Consider the motor/ generator known as ATP Synthase. To give it its proper title it is Adenosine Triphosphate Synthase. Every student of any biological

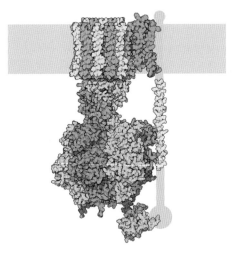

ATP Synthase drawn from structures determined by X-ray crystallography and NMR spectroscopy
(Mitochondrial inner membrane shown schematically in grey)

discipline is soon introduced to the amazing qualities and essential nature of adenosine triphosphate (ATP) in living systems. It is a ubiquitous energy storage molecule and is essential to most active cellular activities, whether permitting movement or the propagation of impulses along nerve fibres or even driving various reactions in the pathways of intermediary metabolism, cell replication and repair – very little happens without ATP. Actually, from a chemical angle, it is a nucleoside triphosphate comprising adenine (a nitrogenous base), ribose (a sugar), and the phosphate moiety. Structurally it is a close relative of one of the precursor subunits of DNA (de-oxyribonucleic acid) or RNA (ribonucleic acid). We'll look in more detail at the nucleic acids later.

As oxygen is being consumed in the process of energy utilisation ATP is converted to either ADP or AMP (the di-phosphate or mono-phosphate byproducts). This is known as de-phosphorylation. In order to recharge the energy source, various metabolic pathways appear designed to re-phosphorylate the AMP and ADP to form the energy rich ATP again, and this process goes on repeatedly and continuously within each living cell. Cells have little organelles called mitochondria, which is where most of this activity is located. The production of ATP can result from carbohydrate metabolism by means of various pathways, including glycolysis, the citric acid cycle, and from fat metabolism by a process known as beta-oxidation. As I think about these reactions, it brings back a chilling memory of undergraduate biochemistry and spending many hours trying to memorise the various intermediate and enzyme driven steps in these pathways. Grim! The fascinating result of these reactions fuels a system of molecular complexes serving to sequentially transfer electrons across (in the case of mammalian cells, along) the constituents of the electron transport chain on the inner layer of the membrane of the mitochondrion. This process releases the energy used to pump protons from the inside of the mitochondrion into the space between the double-layered membrane. This creates an electrochemical gradient. The result of this is that protons flow back across the membrane through the ATP synthase complex and as they do, they enable rotation of the motor that the enzyme uses to generate ATP from ADP and inorganic phosphate.

Now that description is a simplified version of the biochemical detail, but it doesn't end there. Not by a long shot! While the flow through the proton channel drives the ring-like motor anchored within the membrane (the F_0 rotary motor), it also turns a second and linked motor that is connected through an axle-like structure. This second motor (the F_1 rotary motor) actually generates the ATP. The schematic diagrams shown here are derived from X-ray crystallography and NMR spectroscopy. Another technique called cryo-electron microscopy has been used to figure out the entire structure of the enzyme and, interestingly, it seems to be arranged in a dimeric formation with each component held in an acutely angled configuration. This relates to the extensively folded nature of the inner mitochondrial membrane.

ATP synthase is without doubt one of the enigmatic wonders of the molecular world. An enzyme, a molecular motor, an ion pump, and another molecular motor all wrapped together in one amazing nanoscale machine.

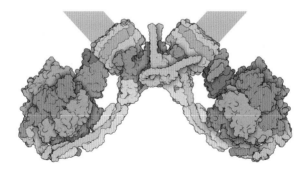

ATP Synthase in dimeric form. The configuration is thought to help shape the extensively folded inner mitochondrial membrane.

The rotary engine is only one variety of the molecular motors, which exist within cells. In fact, cells build three types of ATP-powered motors, myosins, kinesins, and dyneins. Myosins are the impressive proteins used to power our muscles. Muscle cells are stuffed with bundles of actin filaments and these form the cytoskeleton of the muscle cells. These are tiny, typically about 7 nanometres in diameter and sometimes cross-linked in different ways to provide different structures. Myosin uses the energy of ATP to change conformation and position and thus move along the actin to achieve muscle contraction. The structure of the actin is a kind of loose double helical arrangement with specific directional orientation such that the motor protein myosin only actively moves along the filament in one direction. Of course, there is close coordination so that within one muscle fibre the contraction all occurs simultaneously, otherwise little or no useful work would result.

Kinesins and dyneins, on the other hand, walk along microtubules, dragging their cellular cargo along with them. For some cellular processes, because the distances involved are small, the chemical reactions depend on simple diffusion for the delivery of the right substrates. This is how the various molecules involved in glycolysis (part of the oxidative phosphorylation we considered already as one component of the process of providing the right conditions for ATP production) get to the site of the action. There are some ten enzymes

137

involved and the raw material finds its way by randomly charging around within the cell cytoplasm, until it binds and is drawn into the specific part of the process. For small molecules and proteins, random diffusion is fast enough to get the job done, but for some larger tasks, cells have to take a more active approach. This is where the staggering (literally) molecular motors come in.

Typical cells contain an array of microtubules, linear polymers of the protein tubulin, all arrayed in a configuration specific to their function. Each microtubule has a positive and a negative end. Some are orientated from the centre of the cell outwards towards the surface. They can be involved in mitosis and meiosis assisting the movement of nucleic acids into position for cell division. Some are involved in less spectacular intracellular transport, still others are essential to ciliary activity at the cell surface and a proportion is responsible for the cellular shape and structure.

The kinesins are proteins with a cargo binding domain and an engine composed of two feet (strangely enough these are known as heads) that appear to 'walk' step by step along the microtubule, dragging whatever large object is in need of transportation. Cargo such as lysosomes or other vesicles may contain enzymes, constituents of various metabolic or cell signalling reactions, or such secretory products as hormones or neurotransmitters can also be carried in this way. Unbound kinesin is folded up and only when it binds with a cargo load do the heads become free and therefore available to interact with the microtubule. The walking motion is ATP powered, the switch between microtubule binding and unbinding leads to the step by step conformational change, swinging each head forward in turn, steering them electrostatically, thus allowing the kinesin to progress along the tubule towards the positive end and drag its cargo in tow.

Another group of cytoskeletal motor proteins that also ride the rails of the microtubules but in the opposite direction are the dyneins. They are also active in a range of activities including transport and various motor functions required to shift genetic material during cell replication.

Undoubtedly, there is a theoretical mechanism for the emergence and production of machines like these. The problem is that the balance required and the systematised nature of the cooperation between various components again presents us with the same issue. There is no method of manufacturing any complex, multi component, interlocking biological system in a series of small steps which individually confer no functional advantage, and thus the progressive stages are not selectable. No selection. No survival!

Minor adjustments can result from gradual genetic change, but an explanation for machines and systems in our cellular factories demands a different explanation. Some options are now being considered but they are a far cry from the thinking that spawned the so-called modern synthesis of evolutionary thought. We should bear in mind that it is not so modern in the 21st century, having been around since the 1920s. It is obviously not up to the logical burden being placed upon it by our appreciation of the nature of molecular machinery and systems related biology. The new ideas, now coming together in the latest extended evolutionary synthesis, are well worth exploring and we are heading in that direction. We are in good company. The world-renowned Royal Society has been fostering careful consideration in the light of the explanatory deficits of the standard mechanism of evolutionary theory. To give it its full title, the 'Royal Society of London for Improving Natural Knowledge', first came into being in 1660 under the patronage of King Charles II and it is possibly the oldest and most famous scientific society in the world. The concerns we have encountered in a brief tour through some recent biochemical machinery has provided some of the background to encourage a multidisciplinary discussion, seeking a better explanation for the observations such as those we have described. For the past six decades the gene centric understanding has been the reigning paradigm. A different approach with a revised understanding of the role of adaptive variations, epigenetic effects and a whole suite of additional mechanisms beyond mutation, have now been brought to the table and include natural genetic engineering, horizontal gene transfer and a host of others.

Setting the mechanisms aside, however, there is one other area we ought to consider. This will blend the wonders of even more amazing molecular machinery with an additional enigma. If you think the implications of the machine content of sub-cellular systems are far reaching, there is another enigma, which opens an entirely different realm.

Take home message ...

Macromolecular machinery is not an analogy. Protein machines have a clear purpose embedded in their structure. Purpose reflects intentionality and intentionality infers design.

Twisted information

The mission of DNA is to evolve nervous systems capable of deciphering the mission of DNA.

Timothy Leary [1920-1996]

IT WAS EXACTLY TEN YEARS after Charles Darwin published his first edition of *On the Origin of Species by Means of Natural Selection, or the Preservation of Favoured Races in the Struggle for Life* in 1859[24] that the Swiss chemist Frederich Miescher first observed a substance he labelled nuclein which he identified within the nuclei of human white blood cells. Miescher was really chasing the protein constituents of white cells, but he did recognise that this nuclein did not display the typical characteristics of protein. The phosphorous content was much higher than typical proteins and it was resistant to the usual methods of breaking proteins apart. He recognised that he had observed something different. Miescher's name hardly features now but he was sure that he was on to something and possibly something really significant. He wrote, "It seems probable to me that a whole family of such slightly varying phosphorous-containing substances will appear, as a group of nucleins, equivalent to proteins."[25]

It took many more years to figure out exactly how the constituents of DNA were assembled, but the chemical nature gradually became clearer. The Russian biochemist, Phoebus Levene, was the first

141

person to elucidate the arrangement of the three major subunits of a single segment of DNA; a nucleotide, by noting the phosphate, the sugar that he later correctly identified as deoxyribose, and the nitrogenous base. At that stage, the unique arrangement of the sugar-phosphate backbone of the long DNA chain of nucleotides was still a mystery. By the mid 1940s it was agreed that the hereditary qualities of cells were contained in DNA and an Austrian biochemist, Edwin Chargaff, set out to work on the detailed chemistry of the nucleic acids. Reflecting on his experience in 1971[26] he recalled the importance of a paper by Avery from Rockefeller University back in 1944.[27] Considering that publication, which suggested that DNA was the hereditary chemical of bacterial genes, he wrote: "This discovery, almost abruptly, appeared to foreshadow a chemistry of heredity and, moreover, made probable the nucleic acid character of the gene ... Avery gave us the first text of a new language, or rather he showed us where to look for it. I resolved to search for this text."

Chargaff went on to observe that the bases (adenine, guanine, thymine, and cytosine) were not ordered along the molecule in a strictly recurring or predictable way. He did, however, point out that the amount of the purine base, adenine (A), was usually similar to the amount of pyrimidine base, thymine (T), and the same applied for the purine, guanine (G) which was almost identical in quantity to the pyrimidine, cytosine (C).

Work on the physical structure of DNA was progressing by means of X-ray crystallography, and it was sight of the images produced by Maurice Wilkins [1916-2004] and Rosalind Franklin [1920-1958] in 1953, that led James Watson [1928-] and Francis Crick [1916-2004] to propose that the structure of DNA was a double helix. The complementary base pairs are held together by hydrogen bonds; adenine is always paired with thymine and guanine is always paired with cytosine. The major insight leading to the understanding we have of DNA being a repository of genetic information came from Francis Crick again. In 1958 he wrote a paper making the link between the specific base sequences on DNA with the specific amino acid sequence in a protein. It is clear that the exact amino acid sequence is responsible for the shape of the protein as it folds and the shape, in turn, is critical to its function. So this ties the base arrangement to molecular function; the so-called sequence hypothesis. In giving his Nobel Lecture when he, Watson, and Maurice Wilkins were awarded the Nobel Prize for Physiology and Medicine in 1962; the award being made 'for their discoveries concerning the molecular structure of nucleic acids and its significance for information transfer in living material;' it was obvious to Crick that the DNA contained the genetic instructions in the form of a code. At that stage they were already well along the way to figuring out how the code was broken, read and translated into the protein which it specified. A remarkable story altogether!

When I studied biochemistry, I was truly amazed by the chemical mechanisms used by cells to extract energy from various substrates like carbohydrates or fats. Even amino acids can be used in certain circumstances. However, to me, even more amazing by far was the story of DNA replication in preparation for cell division. If the examples of molecular machinery we have considered so far are impressive, and indeed they are, the machinery involved in the process of DNA copying takes us to a different level.

In February 2001, the cover of the journal *Nature* carried an imaginative image and a headline that concealed the great excitement that accompanied the announcement being made in that issue. It had taken some 13 years and cost more than a billion dollars, but the human genome had been fully sequenced! All 3 billion letters! The chemical text or code that Crick had recognised had been released from the length of human DNA and the base pair order had been characterised for the very first time, unlocking the detailed genetic information previously hidden within the double helix.

In order to get at or copy this ordered information, the DNA has to be unwound to expose the purine and pyrimidine bases. An enzyme called topoisomerase accomplishes this. This allows molecular machines called polymerases to match corresponding bases and provides for a complementary strand of DNA to be manufactured.

143

Unwinding the DNA is not an entirely straightforward process. The hydrogen bonds binding the bases together are quite strong and require considerable energy to separate the two strands. This is where the enzyme DNA helicase comes into its own.

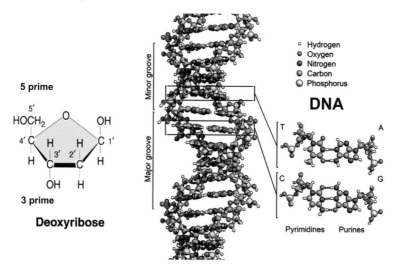

Molecular structure and double helical arrangement of DNA

The diagram shows the arrangement of a short segment of DNA and it is important to note the configuration. When it comes to appreciating the nanotechnology involved in replicating DNA, the orientation is crucial. The two sugar phosphate chains are orientated in opposite directions. The convention here is based on the configuration of the deoxyribose. Each of the five carbon atoms in the pentose monosaccharide (sugar) molecule is numbered 1 through 5. In one DNA strand the direction runs from the 3 prime end to the 5 prime end and the complementary strand runs in the opposite direction.

It would be incorrect to think of helicase as a single entity. In fact, there is a family of helicases built for different conditions and different strand orientations. Essentially, they are motor proteins, fuelled by ATP, some of which progress along the strand from the 3 prime end and some start at the 5 prime end. They are capable of pulling apart the two strands in a DNA double helix at dizzying speed and there is evidence that when they appear to partner with the enzymes involved in copying the new strands of DNA, they work even more quickly.[28] Some estimates suggest that they can process 1,000 base pairs per second. As the base pairs are separated, the site of separation becomes known as a replication fork.

In order to initiate the process of copying the DNA, the key starting point to which the DNA polymerase needs access is the 3 prime end of a strand. The free hydroxyl (OH) group bound to the third carbon atom on the pentose is where the helicase can start strutting its stuff. It accomplishes its task with incredible fidelity and, as it duplicates the genetic code, it is thought to produce a mistake in less than 1 per billion base pairs. It also has the ability to proof read the result and excise an incorrect base repairing the DNA perfectly as it goes.

The sharp-eyed reader will have noticed that as the two strands are separated they are orientated in opposite directions. These strands are called the leading and lagging strands. These strands are created in one direction only - from the 5 prime end to the 3 prime end of the new strand. The polymerase can only add to the 3 prime end of the strand it is building. The leading strand is synthesised continuously in this direction while the lagging strand is synthesised in small segments called Okazaki fragments.

This is necessary because the other strand being orientated the opposite way needs to be presented to the DNA polymerase in an orientation with which it can cope. So the molecular machinery drags out the lagging strand in these loops to allow a break point to be made and DNA polymerase to latch on to the chain and start adding nucleotides to the 3 prime hydroxyl group end, thus constructing the basis for a new, complementary double helical loop. There are various other machines which hold, clamp, re-orientate, split and copy these looped fragments (Okazaki fragments), which, following copying, are rejoined by another machine, DNA ligase. Some wonderful animations have been prepared to demonstrate how this works and it certainly looks even more impressive than a complicated robotic assembly line, such as might be used in car manufacturing for example.[29] Each machine picks up the required stimulus to start, perform its function and move on to the next segment.

We can certainly marvel at the astonishing complexity and efficiency of DNA replication, but beyond the machinery there are at least two levels of mystery. They are not often expressed, perhaps because of their perplexing nature. However we need to face them and see if there are any clues that might help us towards a resolution.

The first conundrum concerns the code and calls for a detailed description while the second concerns the machinery used to read, copy, and translate the code and can be stated very briefly. Let's take them in turn.

It was no surprise that Professor Engström of the Royal Caroline Institute, in making the award ceremony speech for the Nobel Prize in Physiology and Medicine in 1962, recognised both the transmissible code contained within DNA and its far-reaching implications for biology and medicine. A code comprises a set of rules required to convert information from one variety to another. They are generally high-level encrypted languages, characters or symbols that represent something beyond themselves and convey meaning when the code is deciphered. Codes, therefore, can be considered to be replete with specific functional information. So our first puzzle is to try to understand the source of the code. Where does the information come from? DNA has all the features of a code or a language. It is not an analogy of a language; it has all the required characteristics. It has individual characters, the base pairs functioning, as do letters in an alphabet. Furthermore, the letters are arranged in orderly groups that are evidently not random in that they convey meaning. The decoding of the cryptic puzzle makes use of its structure. Just as the interpretation of a typographical language requires rules of spelling and sentence construction to be accurate and effective, so it is with the nucleic acids in the genetic code. They have structured arrangements and are translated for example from DNA to RNA to protein; a progression which came to be known as the central dogma of biology. This essentially connects the coded information in the genes to the physical characteristics of the proteins that are specified by that code. The information can be considered to flow from DNA via RNA to protein but not in the opposite direction. So, in reality, this is an actual language constructed of 4 different purine and pyrimidine base pairs with their own grammar, meaning and intent. Like any other code it communicates, represents or symbolises something beyond itself.

The information loaded in the characteristic genetic material of DNA is, as we have seen, linked to the machinery without which life could not exist. It seems to me that this is the fundamental difference between inanimate and animate matter. The entire living world spends enormous amounts of energy processing information. Cells are positively bristling with receptors, allowing sophisticated mechanisms to continually adjust to the environment, modifying their chemical activity, stimulating various processes such as motility, cell division, and a host of others and making the most appropriate response in all circumstances. The secret of success lies in the ability to assimilate, decode, and make a coherent, purposeful response to the input.

The entire biosphere is bursting with genetic information. It is available to be copied, re-coded, translated, up-regulated, down-regulated, switched on and off and the way this works takes our understanding of molecular production lines to a completely new level.

We appreciate that coded information typically comes from a specific source: usually someone who devised the rules of the code, an author. Such an agent who is responsible for the code design is essential in order that the encrypted message, which appears to be gibberish, might be rendered meaningful when it is processed.

We now appreciate that long stretches of DNA can be copied and right away we, therefore, have a mechanism for generating new

DNA. However, if it is a copy – it hardly counts as new information. We also understand that the copying can, infrequently, be imperfect and so this is a possible route to new information. There are even more exotic ways of generating sophisticated results from the DNA sequences that are in existence within an organism. Cells can exchange chunks of genetic material; a process called horizontal gene transfer. What if the reading framework were to change, different points selected for starting to read and process the code – a frame shift? This would create a completely different set of words and characters and, in effect, result in new information. It is not the way that standard languages work, of course, but with the kind of adaptive and exotic living control mechanisms, it is conceivable, albeit a little far-fetched, that an explanation like this could account for several layers of different information emanating from the same sequence of bases – just that they would be decrypted with a different outcome. In reality genetic messages have been discovered to overlay other messages. Genes can indeed overlap and appear like added layers of new genetic information. In fact, it now looks as though any idea that the nucleic acids were the only information reservoir is simply naïve. It turns out that information is present in all sorts of unexpected places, cell membranes, proteins, and protein–carbohydrate complexes.

What is now becoming clear is that information change, even in the genetic code itself, does not depend only on random alteration of the DNA sequence. It has long been known that DNA copying errors or accidental mutations tend to degrade genetic information and, while there may be no tangible effect on the function of a gene, there are occasions when the gene function is so degraded and broken that the consequences are serious and damaging. There are many examples of such information change, effectively destroying gene function or changing it in such a way as to produce irrevocable changes to function. Think about the analogy of a software programme. Introduce some random changes to the code and the outcome is unlikely to be helpful! Putting it the other way, if one wanted to prepare some new software to accomplish a particular task, the approach to take habitually involves writing new code. Most assuredly the method most likely to fail would be to take some existing code and to start making random changes to the coding language within the software. How could it be that the world of biology has been so wedded to such a dead-end idea for so long?

The notion that the specific information required for specified protein production should depend on random mutations or copying errors, even with the filter of natural selection, is much more likely to produce a non-functioning protein soup than, for example, an enzyme or a functional molecular machine. In trying to make sense of the cause of specific protein coding it should be very clear that it is not possible to re-run an evolutionary process, such as is postulated, to deliver the results we observe. Rather we need to consider different possible causes and evaluate these hypotheses in the light of their plausibility and the degree to which they fit what we actually understand and observe. The standard mechanism of the modern evolutionary synthesis is simply not up to the mark. Whenever we need to account for the cause of a multi-component system like the pituitary or cooperative molecular machinery working together for a particular purpose the modern synthesis just cannot provide the necessary mechanism. So, is there a different or additional route that might rescue the endeavour and provide the infusion of information required? Well, there are a few candidates and it is worth mentioning these because they are the focus of a great deal of current research on this enigma.

Working on bacterial genetics James Shapiro [1943-] from the University of Chicago, has been involved in studying the way genetic information is processed. He described how stretches of code could be copied from one DNA sequence to another, a process called replicative transposition. More recently he has advanced the idea of natural genetic engineering,[30] where environmental changes can affect DNA processing. It is now clear that there are many intracellular mechanisms which appear to facilitate the restructuring of DNA in predictable and systematic ways and these processes, which have

149

the capacity to activate and reorganise the genetic material – the natural genetic engineering mechanisms, may well have important implications for the way organisms change and adapt. Even these methods are unable to solve the problem concerning the source of information. Indeed, they simply compound it. If the natural genetic engineering functions like a pre-programmed adaptive capacity that is built into the organism in some way, it begs the question, what could be the source of the information for this added layer of adaptive, algorithmic control?

Note that this calls the central dogma into some question; indeed it serves to suggest that changes in the proteins, while perhaps not formally transmitting information backwards, nevertheless produce a resulting adaptive effect on the activity and metabolism of the nucleic acids. In fact, having a method of bringing new information algorithms into play could, for example, more adequately account for the rapid changes that may be required for cellular activity such as preparing immune competent cells to respond to a threat or for damaged tissues to mobilise the cellular equipment required to effect damage limitation and repair. Shapiro has illustrated this with multiple examples such as the role of the histone proteins, which package the DNA into ordered structural units, in modifying DNA. There are also examples of ways in which enzymatic activity can modify nucleotides. Genetic elements can move within the genome and these transposons could, theoretically, be responsible for informational change. However, there is plenty of evidence that genome damage is the most likely outcome.

One could suggest that the expression of genetic information is highly regulated and indeed that appears to be the case. There appear to be certain genes that control when other genes are switched on or off. Could it be that the expression of genetic information is managed by the resetting of gene regulatory networks? The problem with this as a potential explanation for new information is that these systems themselves require a high order of specific information so to invoke more and more complex information-rich systems to explain the source of information argues in a circle and solves nothing.

A few years ago, my wife and I travelled to a remote part of the Isle of Lewis in the Outer Hebrides off the West coast of northern Scotland. On the far western coast, Uig features a long sweeping bay with a beautiful, unspoilt sandy beach. Experimenting with social media we uploaded some photographs for friends at home and wrote in sand in enormous letters, the question "Wish you were here?" Only 15 letters but it will be obvious that the message conveyed meaning and anyone reading those words would not for a single second imagine that the source of that message was some random process. Information carrying purpose or meaning habitually comes from a conscious source. For any language of any kind, there is always a mind behind it. So while there may be no question as to the origin of 15 meaningful letters, 19 characters if you include the spaces and the question mark, isn't it odd that we are often quick to assume or even assert that the 3 billion or so letters of the human genome emanate from some accidental, undirected source? Can there be any justification, scientific or otherwise for such a view? We have seen that the genetic code is structured, meaningful, representative, coded language and we know of no natural process that could account for it. It surely calls for a measure of humility in our thinking, especially as there is no precedent, no logic and no known mechanism to account for the origin of biological information.

So, now to our second conundrum and I can state this problem very briefly indeed. It concerns the machinery used to read, copy, and translate the code about which we have been thinking. Given all that has gone before, and recalling the molecular factory required to replicate DNA, it raises the rather obvious question. Which came first? Was it the protein machinery needed to decode the DNA or the DNA template required to manufacture the protein machinery? This takes us even deeper into the cryptic web of life's origin and takes us to a problem that was not lost on Charles Darwin himself. Indeed in the *Origin* he expressed his concern. In the section discussing the 'organs of extreme perfection and complication', he was clearly intrigued as to the function of the eye and pondering photosensitivity, he noted the bigger conundrum which was left hanging, 'How a nerve comes to be sensitive to light hardly concerns us more than how life itself first originated.' Quite so!

Take home message ...

If the characteristics of cellular machinery are not persuasive enough – add the underlying organised information which is an indubitable feature of genetic material. Coded information can only arise from an intentional source.

The Mystery of Life's Origin

Life is an unanswered question, but let's still believe
in the dignity and importance of the question.
Tennessee Williams [1911-1983]

A S A STUDENT I CAN remember flipping through the pages of one of my most treasured textbooks. This was a real investment and the main attraction was that, while it was comprehensive, it was easy to digest because it was very richly illustrated. The title - *Hamilton Bailey's Demonstration of Physical Signs in Clinical Surgery*. It was full of photographs of the most obvious and advanced pathology, the like of which one rarely came across in Western clinical practice. There were enormous growths, horrendous tumours, massive goitres, and weird deformities and I really came to regard it as an example of the kinds of abnormality that might have characterised a previous generation. I would think it took me about an hour of meeting patients in a general outpatient clinic in a rural African Mission Hospital to realise that even the examples illustrated by Hamilton Bailey were a feeble reflection of the kind of abnormalities that were commonplace in the bush. Within a few days I had amassed a collection of clinical photographs with lumps, bumps, tumours, and injuries the like of which would have completely overwhelmed that iconic collection. Spleens which were enormous; just about all of the local population had huge splenic enlargement as a result of infection with a curious little fluke called Schistosoma mansoni. The source is the River Zambezi which was where the local people obtained their water, where they bathed, did their laundry, and even went fishing. The river is central to their very existence, but it also carries horrific dangers. The schistosomes cause an awful chronic condition called schistosomiasis or bilharzia, that has a huge range of additional effects on different systems within the body. Huge splenomegaly is one obvious telltale sign of infection. Unrelated to this, there were also goitres bigger than I have ever seen, dermoid cysts, dentigerous cysts, ovarian cysts, lymphomas, jaw tumours and abdominal masses, any or all of which would have easily outgunned those deemed impressive enough to gain a place in Hamilton Bailey's collection. On one memorable ward round I came across four different patients who had sustained bites of various kinds involving four different species. All of them had sustained tissue loss (a posh way of saying that parts of their anatomy were severely damaged or even missing). One from a snake bite, another from a crocodile attack, and these were relatively common, a third from a human bite and, perhaps most remarkably, given the patient was still a live patient and not a corpse, the final one from a hippopotamus bite! It did occur to me that clinical practice in Africa would be much different if there were rather more inter-species respect and if they could desist from biting one another!

One day George rolled in, dressed in prison garb and chained to two rather surly prison guards. For him, life in this remote corner of rural Zambia had taken a significant downturn. In a moment of kindness, or maybe weakness, he had agreed to guarantee a debt for his brother and essentially act as bondsman for him. When the brother skipped off with no thought of the risk for his kind sibling, poor George was arrested and imprisoned in the local jail. Not the most salubrious accommodation as you might imagine. There was however one small benefit. As a guest of the government there was at least the possibility of some access to healthcare. Now George had been suffering from an increasingly troublesome and even embarrassing problem; he had terrible hyperhidrosis affecting both hands. This is a rare condition, but it can be extremely irksome and inconvenient. The symptoms are distressing and result from a dramatic overproduction of sweat in the hands, which made it very difficult for George to grip anything and certainly difficult to hold down a job. You could actually watch and see the fluid dripping from his hands. Objects literally slipped through his fingers. I had seen a few such cases over my years of practising surgery in the UK but this case was more severe than anything I had come across before. There are various medical treatments but, to be honest, few of them are of much use. There is, however, an amazing surgical approach which can cure this condition. The downside is that it involves the need to get access to the autonomic nerves in the upper part of the chest. The sympathetic chain courses alongside the spine and it can be clearly seen inside the thoracic cavity as it courses over the necks of the ribs all the way down. The minor problem, of course, is how to get access and obtain that view from the inside. In the UK the answer is not too difficult. A camera connected to a rigid telescope known as a thoracoscope can throw the internal image on a high definition video screen and the surgeon simply has to deflate the lung to gain a good view of the sympathetic chain. The critical part of the surgery to correct hyperhidrosis is to ensure that the chain is divided at exactly the right level, ideally between the second and third thoracic segments. The lung can then be re-inflated and the wounds repaired. The procedure has to be repeated on the other side to get the bilateral effect. Achieving the desired effect of disconnecting the autonomic drive to sweat production in the palms is usually not too difficult, however if the cut is made too high, say above the level of the neck of the second rib, you can end up causing Horner's syndrome. When that happens the patient will have an obvious droopy eyelid, a constricted pupil, and will likely lose sweat production from the same side of the face. So there is an element of pressure on the surgeon; get it wrong and the chances are that the patient will suffer and everyone else will see that all is not well!

For George, I did my best to explain the proposed treatment to him. He had quite a good command of English so was able to give consent. I have no doubt that it was informed consent, but I am also sure that he was sceptical about the tale I was telling him about burning two small nerves in his chest and the result would be two dry hands! I could see what he was thinking – it was a "Give me a break!" moment. We've all had them when something seems so improbable that it is hard to believe. Are you really telling me that if you stick a camera in my chest and use an electric current to burn some funny nerves in my back that my hands will become dry? He had a kind of incredulous look that communicated an unspoken thought that the tale was beyond anything he was prepared to really believe or accept.

For whatever reason, perhaps the risk of the surgery and a short hospital stay outweighed the prospect of doing the time in Zambezi jail. Being Africa, we did have some technical difficulties with the telescope and were unable to generate an image on the video monitor, so the surgery was completed using the old fashioned technique of putting the camera up to the eye. It did mean that I had to become a kind of operating contortionist both to see what I was doing and accomplish the nerve division. Despite the concept being hard for George to believe, after his surgery he left hospital and went back to jail, very happy because both hands were completely dry for the first time in several years. The sceptical glance had been replaced by a huge smile!

Now, it would be true to say that we've struggled to specify exactly what distinguishes the animate from the inanimate, although I hope you agree that we have come close with our discussion of biological information. Before we can even logically reach the issues relating to the diversity and complexity of life forms we need to move back a step. Before biological change could even take place, before environmental conditions could favour one particular variant over another, life itself had to get up and running.

Life at its most basic level is fancy chemistry. What distinguishes it from other forms of fancy chemistry is not only the presence of the underlying information, but also what happens as a result of processing that information. The combined effect supports cellular life, which self organises, self sustains, self repairs, and self replicates, but remarkably, it also produces independent free-living organisms. Creatures such as humans, fancy chemistry for sure, but chemistry from which emerges the ability to decide for itself, look after itself, preserve itself and even enquire about itself: how did it come to be? And more perplexing still: Why?

There is no argument about how sophisticated we are. In fact, we are a good deal more sophisticated than we appreciate. The overarching scientific question, that currently appears to be an insoluble mystery, is how the first life got started. From a purely natural point of view, there are various stories purporting to describe how organic chemicals might have been formed and if the circumstances were peculiarly favourable how they might have aggregated together in some way and perhaps even developed the capacity to replicate themselves. Furthermore, the story goes, not only did these complicated chemicals self-assemble into ever advancing communities, but they were also able to protect themselves within a membranous barrier, allowing even more elaborate metabolic activity to arise in a more protected and concentrated system.

Can we genuinely hope that this kind of tale is likely to be close to the truth? I think not. I have always been attracted to chemistry; indeed, it was an interest in chemistry that drew me towards a career in medicine. Pharmaceutical chemistry, pharmacology, and therapeutics are important and fascinating components of a physician's armoury. Mind you, surgery is a bit of a conceptual shift again and that is where I ended up. Rather unkindly, the anaesthesiologist with whom I worked many years was always keen to point out where the blood brain barrier was in the operating room! Furthermore, decrying my knowledge of chemical pharmacology, if I was ever to ask him to give a particular antibiotic or vasoactive drug, he frequently announced to any visitors or observers present that any surgeon with a working knowledge of more than two drugs had no right to call himself (or herself) a consultant. Maybe he had a fair point.

Nevertheless, in discussion with a friend who worked in synthetic physical chemistry whilst researching his PhD project, he often spoke of how fiendishly difficult it was to manufacture a particular molecule in the lab. Even if you know the formula and have all the equipment you might need for the process; the business of obtaining completely pure substrates, controlling the speed and efficiency of the reactions that need to take place, characterising the result and confirming that you have produced what you set out to produce is not, in any way, simple or straightforward. We have already observed how incredibly complex and detailed are the molecular machines and information storage systems we have been considering so far. The prebiotic chemical constituents required for life to get going include sugars, fats, amino acids, and, of course, nucleic acids. That is just the beginning because none of these are found in only their simplest forms but, as we have seen, they combine in complicated systems and communities, cooperating, interacting, and regenerating with astonishing capacity and efficiency. I have often really wondered how on earth all of that could possibly occur spontaneously. Yet that is the position being assumed. For the methodological naturalist, any real design is off the table and life must have emerged by some purely spontaneous physical and chemical process. Really?

We have already addressed the difficulty of sourcing the code to drive the entire endeavour. Beyond that, think for a moment about the membranes required to enclose the cellular chemistry workshops. Mammalian cell membranes are composed of a lipid bilayer. When James Tour, who is a celebrated and innovative synthetic organic chemist, thought about membrane structure he seriously challenged the idea that just because lipid bilayers can form spontaneously from lipids of a particular length, membranes could therefore emerge from some spontaneous process. He was careful to add that, while

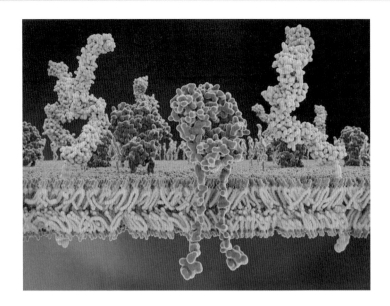

the 'simple' structure of a lipid bilayer might be a reasonable starting point, in fact there are myriads of different lipid structures within cell membranes.[31] He lists glycerolipids, sphingolipids, sterols, prenols, saccharolipids, and polyketides and the addition of any of these may well de-stabilise a bilayer membrane. He further pointed out that the outer and inner surfaces have their distinctive and specific characteristics and the lipid structure is just the start. He goes on, 'Protein–lipid complexes are the required passive transport sites and active pumps for the passage of ions and molecules through bilayer membranes, often with high specificity. Some allow passage for substrates into the compartment, and others their exit. The complexity increases further because all lipid bilayers have vast numbers of polysaccharide (sugar) appendages, known as glycans, and the sugars are no joke. These are important for nanosystem and microsystem regulation. The inherent complexity of these saccharides is daunting. Six repeat units of the saccharide D-pyranose can form more than one trillion different hexasaccharides through branching (constitutional) and glycosidic (stereochemical) diversity. Imagine the breadth of the library!'

What is his ultimate point? It is surely this. It is evident that to produce a cell, even a simple cell, if that is not itself a contradiction, one would need all the chemical constituents, all the sugars and salts, the nucleic acids, the lipids and amino acids, and they would need to be present in exactly the right concentrations with the correct stereo-chemical configuration. Not only that, there would need to be an incredibly favourable environment (whether it may be close to an undersea hydrothermal vent or some other 'warm little pond') together with some, as yet unidentified, physical push to encourage the molecules to come together and assemble into thousands of integrated nano-systems, the ion pumps, the replication and protein manufacturing machinery, the cytoskeleton, the sensing and signalling mechanisms to mention just a few. Sound like a challenge? You'd better believe it! Tour has written an interesting article about this very issue and without putting words in his mouth; his derision about the optimism of the pre-biotic chemistry theorists is palpable. He considers several steps that would need to be just right. The correct reagents in pure and stereo chemically specific form, the preparation of the necessary sugars; a formidable problem, the virtual impossibility of controlling reactions in water, the stable polymerisation of nucleic acids, and the complexity of the proteoglycan components. To claim that the macromolecules ever assembled spontaneously, is an assertion wildly divorced from any mechanism we can envisage. To hold the even more demanding belief by affirming that 'all subcellular subsystems could have arisen simultaneously through common chemistry' is simply delusional.[32]

To claim that we have a set of mechanisms which can plausibly account for complex biochemistry, far less cells and organelles with specific, information-rich, lipid bilayer membranes, amounts to little more than fanciful storytelling. It should be evident that the chance of that happening is so vanishingly small, that even to entertain the idea that this is what happened is so preposterous as to be disconnected from reality. I feel like saying "Give me a break!"

If an organic synthetic chemist like Tour has an issue, my anxiety about believing the assertion that this is what happened at the origin of first life feels perfectly justified. If you want to sell me that idea, just as George was incredulous about sympathectomy until the evidence was in, I am deeply suspicious of this story about abiogenesis. No scientist, synthetic chemist or origin of life researcher, has come remotely close to demonstrating that life somehow emerged from non-living material. The assumption or the mantra that it 'just happened' spontaneously is so preposterous that I cannot understand how anyone with a mere smattering of physical or chemical knowledge would be prepared to buy the idea.

We are driven these days by the same imperative that holds in the natural sciences and that is, that a credible theory or hypothesis ought to have an evidence base. When we postulate a mechanism which not only does not have such an evidence base, but in reality demands that we discard the evidence we have already accumulated, that mechanism must be rejected as unsupportable.

It may be, of course, that there is an alternative reason why people might be willing to place a bet on something that their head tells them is impossible and it is the irrational idea concerning the possible alternative. We have not really expressed it clearly so far, but if the origin of life is not explained by any physical mechanism, we clearly need an alternative offering. Could it be that the cosmos and life arose by the influence of some designing agency? Now right away, whenever such a radical idea is floated, the scientific world calls "Foul!" For the methodological naturalist, the only available mechanisms would be entirely natural; physical and chemical. Notice that the concern is not so much about the truth of the matter but rather the options need to be constrained to exclude possibilities that are not thought to be palatable.

Consider this from the evolutionary biologist Richard Lewontin. Writing a review of Carl Sagan's *Demon Haunted World: Science as a Candle in the Dark*, he admitted, "Our willingness to accept scientific claims that are against common sense is the key to an understanding of the real struggle between science and the supernatural. We take the side of science in spite of the patent absurdity of some of its constructs, in spite of its failure to fulfil many of its extravagant promises of health and life, in spite of the tolerance of the scientific community for unsubstantiated just-so stories, because we have a prior commitment, a commitment to materialism. It is not that the methods and institutions of science somehow compel us to accept a material explanation of the phenomenal world, but, on the contrary, that we are forced by our a priori adherence to material causes to create an apparatus of investigation and a set of concepts that produce material explanations, no matter how counter-intuitive, no matter how mystifying to the uninitiated. Moreover, that materialism is absolute, for we cannot allow a Divine Foot in the door." [33]

If ever I came across a science 'just so' story, the idea that life originated by the right chemicals coming together in an entirely undirected natural process has to be one of the most preposterous.

Take home message ...

A natural spontaneous explanation for life's origin runs against everything we know and understand about how the world operates. There is no hint of a credible undirected mechanism which could come close to explaining the construction of a living cell.

Solving the mystery; what's on the table?

These are my final words on advocacy. If you have the facts on your side, hammer the facts. If you have the law on your side, hammer the law. If you have neither the facts nor the law, hammer the table.

Old legal aphorsism

Paul Davies [1946-] is both an internationally acclaimed physicist and a writer with an amazing output. He is evidently someone who is intrigued by the very mystery we have been considering. He keeps returning to the unsolved problem of the origin of life. In fact, he has tried to confront it in a few different titles and in his most recent book[34] he ties in the central role of information. He suggests that any laws capable of explaining the origin of life must be radically different from scientific laws known to date. Actually, it doesn't really get us much further down the track towards solving the enigma after all. My sense of the mystery is that it remains, and that Davies' sub-title (*How Hidden Webs of Information Are Finally Solving the Mystery of Life*) is somewhat overoptimistic. In a previous offering,[35] he also tackled life's origin. His analysis of the kinds of explanations available to science here were helpful and informative. Let me try to repackage them.

He pointed out that there are, basically, only two kinds of explanations that apply in the natural sciences. One is that the cause of what we can observe, in this case, life, is merely the action of natural law. The other possible explanation is that the cause has been entirely the result of a happy accident.

Actually, the role of serendipity has been behind a number of celebrated medical discoveries. The term originally came from a letter written by the aristocrat and politician, Horace Walpole, the son of the first British Prime Minister. He referred to the tale of the Three Princes of Serendip, the eventual English translation of an original Persian fairy story, Serendip being the ancient Persian name for Sri Lanka. Apparently the three princes were able to determine the location of a missing camel as a result of a series of 'accidents and sagacity', and Walpole invented the term 'serendipity' to refer to an unexpected, fortunate turn of events.

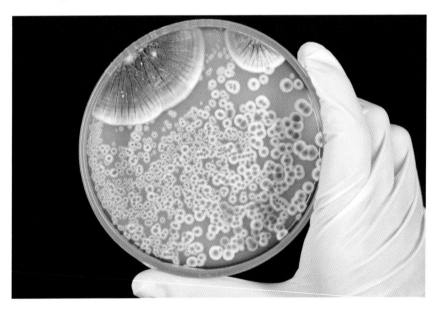

Take, for example, the discovery of penicillin. In the summer of 1928, Alexander Fleming [1881-1955], the Scottish physician and microbiologist, had been off on holiday. He had been working on the organisms thought to be responsible for wound infections and indeed on the counter intuitive problem that antiseptic agents seemed to make things worse rather than better. Apparently he left some culture plates growing bacteria on a bench in the corner of the lab. On returning to his somewhat untidy workspace, he noticed that some of his cultures of a family of bacteria known as staphylococci had become contaminated by a fungal overgrowth. The curious and serendipitous finding was that in those culture plates the bacterial cultures had been killed. He had the presence of mind to take this further and not only identified the mould (Penecillium) but was able to isolate the agent responsible for killing off the staphylococci. Having accidentally discovered penicillin, it eventually went into mass production and revolutionised the treatment of infections.

More recently there was a serendipitous discovery that transformed the treatment of common gastric and duodenal ulcers. When I was at medical school, ulcers were extremely common, in fact just about every single general surgical operating list would have more than one patient having a procedure to reduce the production of acid from the stomach, because that was considered to be the most important causal factor for ulcer disease. In 1982, Barry Marshall [1951-] an Australian postgraduate trainee in clinical medicine was working in the Royal Perth Hospital together with the pathologist Robin Warren [1937-] and together they were intrigued by the appearance of spiral shaped bacteria found in the lining of the stomach in biopsy material from patients shown to have evidence of inflammation in the stomach lining. They were able to isolate the organism which was later called Helicobacter pylori and helped derive a very clever diagnostic test to demonstrate its presence, without necessarily resorting to invasive procedures and the taking of tissue samples. It is now recognised as the most significant causal factor in gastritis, ulcer disease, and gastric cancer, and the mechanism by which it has these effects has been well worked out by means of painstaking detective work. Marshall and Warren were awarded the Nobel Prize for Physiology and Medicine in 2005.

So, maybe we should be cautious before dismissing either the reach of natural law or serendipity, or perhaps a combination of the two, as viable explanations for the enigma of life's origin. Let me take the discussion just a little further to see if such explanations really could be viable after all.

There now exists the notion that serendipity can maybe do the business in allowing life to get started. Jeremy England [1982-] is a physicist at MIT and he had argued that when energy is available to a system of basic chemicals, there is a tendency for these atoms and molecules to group and structure themselves in such a way as to acquire one of the key attributes of living things, namely capturing energy from the environment and dissipating that energy as heat. His paper is pretty technical but basically seems to suggest that since certain chemicals, when subjected to a source of external energy, can produce heat energy into the surroundings, this would be amplified by a mechanism of self-replication. His idea is that this process tends to self-perpetuate, providing the energy source is available, and so matter inexorably and inevitably acquires the very characteristics we associate with living systems. When interviewed by *Quanta Magazine*[36] he was quoted as saying in a rather throwaway fashion that "You start with a random clump of atoms, and if you shine light on it for long enough, it should not be so surprising that you get a plant."

I don't know about you, but the most polite thing I can say about this is that it is an extrapolation way beyond the bounds of his ideas. James Tour is a little more blunt, "The interactions of light with small molecules is well understood. The experiment has been performed. The outcome is known. Regardless of the wavelength of the light, no plant ever forms. We synthetic chemists should state the obvious. The appearance of life on earth is a mystery. We are nowhere near solving this problem. The proposals offered thus far to explain life's origin make no scientific sense."[31]

To invoke the natural laws that we observe at work in the world requires that we properly understand just what they may be able to achieve. Davies makes the point, and we have demonstrated this very clearly already, that life in all its complexity needs not just an explanation for its complex nature but also for the specific information; the code which permeates nucleic acids and indeed a number of other information bearing structures in living systems.

The effect of a natural law can certainly account for some specific and characteristic patterns we may identify in the natural world. For example, the basic laws involved in physics and chemistry can explain the complex nature of the repetitive pattern we might see in a salt crystal, or the specific patterns that might characterise a snowflake, or that might be apparent in a weather system. What those natural laws fail to explain would be the exact ordering of letters in a language, or base pairs in a gene. They could, given the right conditions, explain the formation of a nucleic acid molecule, but specifically cannot account for the meaningful arrangement of the code. The order is not determined by the nature of the chemical bonding, or the relative concentrations in the solution or system in which the molecule is produced – law can't achieve that level of purposeful detail. Laws can produce specific patterns but fall short of achieving specified complexity.

The effect of a lucky break or an accidental occurrence, however, can maybe help to explain complexity. A technical term for an undirected chance occurrence, whether serendipitous or not, is the term 'contingency'. Contingency or random chance could certainly account for complex arrangements of components in a string of bases within DNA. If we were to sequence a randomly assembled length of a nucleic acid, the result would appear complex, maybe extremely complex. But it would be random and not meaningful. It could not be considered to be coded in any way.

So to summarise, Davies explains that contingency, a fluke, can explain complexity but not specification, and natural law can explain specification but not complexity. As he puts it, "Living organisms are mysterious not for their complexity per se, but for their tightly specified complexity."[35] He further explained, "A functional genome is **both** random and highly specific - properties that seem almost contradictory. It must be random to contain substantial amounts of information, and it must be specific for that information to be biologically relevant. Could a law on its own, without a huge element of luck (i.e. chance), do such a thing? Could the genome be the guaranteed product of a deterministic, mechanical, law-like process, like a primordial soup left to the mercy of familiar laws of physics and chemistry? No, it couldn't. No known law of nature could achieve this…"

Maybe there is another genuine alternative explanation. We have already seen that the genetic code shares exactly the characteristics we find in a meaningful language. Think about it this way. If we have a long string of randomly assorted letters and lay them out, the appearance will be one of complete gibberish. Each individual letter is specific but not complex. The string of gibberish is complex but not specific. If you arrange the letters such as I have typed out the string of individual specified letters in this paragraph, it is both complex and specified and, more importantly, meaningful. The string of characters represents something beyond itself. It is a code and conveys purpose to anyone able to decode it. Clearly, any meaningful text has a conscious source and usually an identifiable purpose. It is designed that way. Could it be that the complex specified arrangement of base pairs in protein coding DNA is also the result of real design? It is certainly a potential explanation that meets the requirements where the regular natural explanations completely fail. It is not hard to conclude that there must be an additional explanation that goes beyond and outguns contingency and natural law. Despite it being hard to justify, serendipity has a seat at the origin of life table. It is surely the case that teleology also deserves a place.

Isn't it interesting where you end up with some innocent questions? Here we are reaching some fundamental issues. Starting, as we did in clinical medicine, reaching back into physiology, appealing then to the biochemical wonders of molecular factories and transport systems, we attempted to make some sense of where it all began. We have failed so far to reach a convincing explanation, although we can be pretty confident about some of the popular explanations that can be categorically ruled out.

Before I attempt to bring the entire discussion towards a conclusion, there is another excursion to take, another deeply mysterious and perplexing area to explore and we should go there now before coming to any conclusions. Let me introduce you to some of the most troublesome riddles in neuroscience.

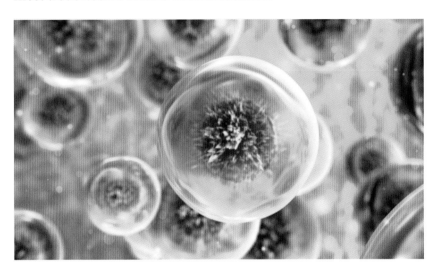

Take home message ...

Contingency can explain complexity but not specification and natural law can explain specification but not complexity. We need both!

Section 3

Thinking about Thinking

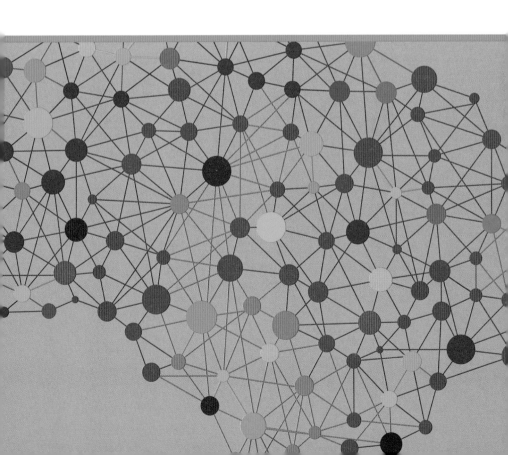

Levels of awareness and what it is like to be me

I F I GO BACK AS far as I possibly can to my earliest memories, only a few incidents are indelibly imprinted and have, so far at least, been impossible to forget. At the age of 5, I can remember two distinct and quite unrelated incidents and would prefer not to have either of them repeated in any form.

The first was finding myself in serious trouble with my parents because, whilst exploring the town centre of an unfamiliar town on Scotland's west coast, I managed to shake off the elderly aunt who was charged with my care and made off under my own steam, to try to find my way back to the house where my parents were located. Success! At least, short-lived success. There was a certain initial sense of achievement, but it was soon punctured with the realisation that the elderly aunt had been abandoned. She did finally make an appearance, having searched high and low for me and, all the while, deeply concerned for my safety. So a significant life lesson was learned the hard way.

The second incident would hopefully never be repeated now, at least not in most Western societies. I was the recipient of a general anaesthetic in a dentist's chair; administered, as was the tradition, by a suitably experienced local general practitioner. It is not a surprise that such dental anaesthesia gained a notorious reputation, as a result of a series of bad outcomes. It is good that it has been consigned to history. Whilst I survived, I can clearly remember the succession of unpleasant experiences leading up to the loss of consciousness. There was the rubbery smell of the mask that was firmly clamped over my face, followed by the addition of a nauseating and strangely sweet but powerful smell of the chloroform. I can clearly recall the sensation that my head was getting bigger and bigger and I guess I then lost consciousness fairly quickly. When I see the easy time that patients now have with the modern intravenous agents that can provide a safe and user-friendly general anaesthetic, I just wish the more civilised approach had been available back then – it would have spared me one of the most unpleasant experiences of my life. Memories are strange and enigmatic phenomena.

I have seen countless patients receive their anaesthetic agents over years in surgical practice. Having an inadequately sedated patient, moving or even wriggling, on the operating table is a profound inconvenience and most surgeons are, understandably, rather intolerant of such circumstances! Anaesthesia has completely transformed surgical practice and I can only imagine how awful it must have been to face surgical trauma without the luxury of total insensibility.

When the Massachusetts General Hospital was opened in 1821, its operating theatre was located in the main Bullfinch Building. It had been a dentist, Horace Wells, who first started regularly using laughing gas (nitrous oxide) in his practice. The gas was responsible for inducing a kind of euphoria and its intoxicating effects made it a popular recreational agent in the nineteenth century. Wells had attended a demonstration given by a showman, Gardner Quincy Colton, who had rolled into town in December 1844, and Wells had been deeply impressed. He immediately saw the potential for benefit by harnessing these effects in dental practice, and the very next day he self-administered some nitrous oxide and had a colleague extract one of his own teeth. He was convinced! There had been no pain and so he rapidly adopted the use of nitrous oxide in his own practice. He then set up a demonstration of his own at the Bullfinch Building with the help of a colleague, William Morton, who was contracted there. Things did not go exactly according to plan. Having heralded this wonderful and life-changing new approach to pain control during dental extraction, the unfortunate and embarrassing result was that the patient cried out in pain during the procedure. The observers, mainly students, seated in the steep banked gallery within the operating room were not impressed. Jeers of "Humbug" were heard and Wells was profoundly discouraged.

Horace Wells' story is a rather tragic one and the subsequent events were extremely sad and unfortunate. Remaining convinced of the potential benefits of complete pain control he became his own subject in the trial of various other chemicals and therein may lie, in part at least, the explanation for his personality change, mental illness, and ultimate suicide. In the meantime, his colleague William Morton was carrying out his own investigations and happened on the effective use of diethyl ether, delivered by a kind of inhaler of his own design. A further demonstration was arranged[37] and this time the willing patient was Gilbert Abbott [1825-1855]. He had been aware of a congenital swelling on the left side of his neck. It was considered to be a vascular malformation; essentially a complex of enlarged blood vessels, although understandably there was, and remains, some dispute about the actual diagnosis. In any event, after a short delay Morton's etherizer was ready and with the help of Harvard Professor of Surgery, Henry Jacob Bigelow, the operating surgeon John Collins Warren prepared to perform the procedure on October 16th 1846. Again, the galleries of the domed operating theatre were filled with eager and curious observers. Abbott began to breathe the ether vapor and was unconscious within a few minutes. Warren made an incision and removed a portion of the swelling from his neck and at the conclusion of the procedure, when fully awake, Abbot confirmed that he had experienced no discomfort, Warren famously pronounced the verdict, "Gentlemen, this is no humbug!"

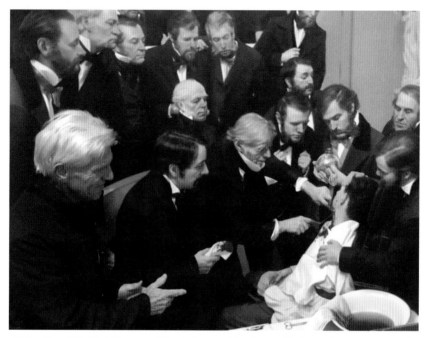

'Ether Day 1846' by Warren and Lucia Prosperi (with an added 21st Century imposter)

A wonderful testimonial for the patient was provided by one of the eyewitnesses and it is worth recording. Washington Ayer [1823-1899] was a medical student at Harvard and was present in the main operating room to witness the demonstration. He later wrote: "Here the most sublime scene ever witnessed in the operating room was presented when the patient placed himself voluntarily upon the table, which was to become the altar of future fame. The heroic bravery of the man who voluntarily placed himself upon the table, a subject for the surgeon's knife, should be recorded and his name enrolled upon parchment, which should be hung upon the walls of the surgical amphitheatre in which the operation was performed. His name was Gilbert Abbott." That operating theatre is no longer used as such but is now the arena in which clinical meetings and so-called Grand Rounds are held. The room became known as the Ether Dome and is now a museum open to visitors. Several paintings commemorate the event and the version by Warren and Lucia Prosperi 'Ether Day 1846' hangs in the Ether Dome itself – I could not resist the temptation to join the team when I visited!

One of the most difficult problems in medicine has been to develop an agreed transferable means of accurately assessing the degree of impairment of awareness or consciousness in patients following, for example, head injury or indeed any other condition which can affect brain function. The same applies to patients following strokes or intracranial bleeds, or those suffering the effects of sepsis or drug use. Two of my senior colleagues in Glasgow, Professors Bryan Jennett and Graham Teasdale, have the distinction of developing a method of doing this simply and reliably. Their method was initially published in 1974[38] and is now in use on every continent, and in the vast majority of hospitals worldwide. It is known as the Glasgow Coma Scale and basically there are three component responses to stimulation that are used to make an assessment. These relate to eye movement, the best motor (movement) response and the best verbal response. Not only does the level of consciousness carry prognostic information for particular clinical scenarios, it is most useful to monitor progress and recognise change, even subtle change, in a patient's condition. While levels of awareness or impairment of some higher mental functions have now been systematised, the actual qualitative experience of awareness is an entirely different matter.

Coming round from a general anaesthetic, where conscious awareness has been switched off, is interesting to observe. As awareness is regained you can sense the improving functional capacity. Patients will begin to move, make eye movements and perhaps show awareness of the discomfort associated with any device used to maintain their airway. Depending on the drugs that have been used and the speed of recovery, they will typically begin to gag, perhaps utter some incomprehensible sounds, respond to the light, grimace or object to their surroundings. Eventually they demonstrate orientation, awareness and regain coherent speech. All of these features can be described and recognised but there is one aspect of this process that cannot be measured or properly delineated and that is the sense of what it is actually like to be conscious. Being conscious has a certain subjective feel to it. It is what it is like to be aware, to note the detail of the movie that seems to run inside our mind. That phenomenon, the feeling of what it is like to be me, from an internal perspective is actually quite difficult to communicate adequately.

Not infrequently the recovery of that accurate internal perception of consciousness remains impaired even after someone has apparently fully recovered from anaesthesia. It is extremely common to identify the characteristic feature of delirium, particularly in postoperative elderly patients who sometimes appear to be 'away with the fairies' – confused and disorientated with impaired cognition and mood disturbances. These features can take several days to settle. Within neuroscience, there is a growing interest in this area. There are some elements of this process that appear to be accessible to attempts to figure out what is going on, others are shrouded in mystery.

The human brain is the most complicated organ that we have ever encountered. Within a single brain there are more connections and junctions than all the devices connected to the World Wide Web. It

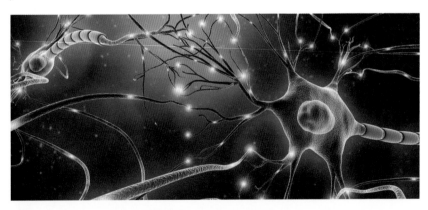

has been estimated that there are around 85 billion neurons in each brain, although the truth may be nearer a figure in excess of 105 billion.[39] Neurons can have thousands and thousands of connections to other neurons so it should not be surprising that estimates of the number of connections or synapses runs to trillions, maybe even in the quadrillion range. The complexity of the brain is virtually unfathomable.

Despite that, huge progress has been made in mapping brain function. For years it took careful correlation of brain injuries or post mortem features with clinical features to try to figure out which parts of the brain were responsible for particular motor or sensory functions. The link between psychological characteristics and certain anatomical locations is also now widely recognised.

One of the early insights came from a most dramatic trauma case; the tale of the celebrated, yet tragic, Phineas Gage. In 1848 at the age of 25, Gage was a railroad foreman and had been hired with his crew to clear some obstructive rock from the intended route of the Rutland and Burlington Railroad, near the small town of Cavendish in Windsor County, Vermont. As team leader, Gage had the responsibility of setting the gunpowder charges and after the blasting holes had been prepared, his role was to sprinkle in some powder, tamp it down gently, at first, and then pack the hole with clay or sand. He was then required to pack the mixture down hard, in order to restrict and control the effect of the explosion. Quite what caused the spark leading the explosive black powder to ignite is not clear. The metre long, 6kg, tamping iron which was slightly narrower at the top, was blown out of the hole and entered Gage's skull underneath his left zygoma, the arch of bone which forms part of the cheekbone, destroying an upper molar tooth and passing behind the left eye as it headed upwards. It followed a track through the cranial cavity traversing the left frontal lobe of the brain and exiting the skull at the top, close to the midline. This was a truly horrendous injury. Other members of his crew told that the tamping iron landed about 25 paces away and stuck upright in the ground. It was streaked with blood and was greasy to the touch! Incidentally, it is notable that he would have scored a full house on the Glasgow Coma Scale as he was walking and talking within a few minutes and even made his way into a cart to be taken back to Cavendish.

The railway doctor was John Harlow and he was quickly on the scene to attend to Gage. He recorded the details, including the diagnostic action he took which would not really be recommended today. It was published in the *Boston Medical and Surgical Journal*.[40] "The accident occurred on 13 September last at 4 o'clock pm. The tamping iron had taken a direction upwards and backwards towards the median line, penetrating the integuments, the masseter and temporal muscles, passing under the zygomatic arch and (probably) fracturing the temporal portion of the sphenoid bone, and the floor of the orbit of the left eye, entering the cranium, passing through the anterior left lobe of the cerebrum and making its exit along the median line, at the junction of the coronal and sagittal sutures, lacerating the longitudinal sinus, fracturing the parietal and frontal bones extensively, breaking up considerable portions of brain, and protruding the globe of the left eye from its socket, by nearly one half of its diameter ... I am informed that the patient was thrown on his back and gave a few convulsive motions of the extremities but spoke in a few minutes ... I did not arrive at the scene of the accident till 6 o clock pm ... assisted by my friend Dr Williams ... I passed in the index finger its whole length without the least resistance in the direction of the wound in the cheek, which received the other finger in a like manner. A portion of the anterior superior angle of each parietal lobe, and a semicircular piece of frontal bone, were fractured, leaving a circular opening of about 3 inches in diameter ... the iron which was found some rods distance, smeared with brain ..."

Despite his apparent escape, not surprisingly he soon fell victim to some infective complications accompanied by an impairment in his conscious level and the prognosis looked grim. However, once again, he beat the odds and survived and, while there is not much clinical evidence to support the exaggerated narrative associated with him,

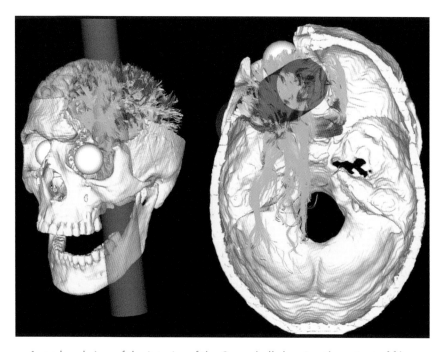

A rendered view of the interior of the Gage skull showing the extent of fibre pathways intersected by the tamping iron

there is some. His case was widely reported to show evidence of profound personality change although how severe, and how durable that change turned out to be, is a matter of doubt.

Dr. Henry Bigelow who was the Head of Surgery in Harvard, and who was present in the Ether Dome to witness the first general anaesthetic demonstration, brought Gage to Harvard and even presented him to professional colleagues as a clinical curiosity. You might be close to the truth in suspecting that surgeons are not necessarily the most acute observers of the more subtle aspects of psychological medicine, but Bigelow reckoned that Gage was 'quite recovered' in his faculties both physically and mentally. Not everyone agreed and while there are many conflicting reports the only other physician with any opportunity for continuing care of Gage was Harlow.

181

In 1868, Harlow recorded some of the 'mental manifestations' resulting from the damage in an issue of the *Bulletin of the Massachusetts Medical Society* as follows, "His contractors, who regarded him as the most efficient and capable foreman in their employ previous to his injury, considered the change in his mind so marked that they could not give him his place again. He is fitful, irreverent, indulging at times in the grossest profanity (which was not previously his custom), manifesting but little deference for his fellows, impatient of restraint or advice when it conflicts with his desires, at times pertinaciously obstinent, yet capricious and vacillating, devising many plans of future operation, which are no sooner arranged than they are abandoned in turn for others appearing more feasible. In this regard, his mind was radically changed, so decidedly that his friends and acquaintances said he was 'no longer Gage.'"

The details of Gage's life after his accident are not well recorded. It is evident that he spent several years driving a team of horses as a coach driver and had a similar job for a while in Chile. Unfortunately his health did not hold up and he came back to the USA in 1859, and clearly suffered from post-traumatic epilepsy. He died in San Francisco in 1860 as a result of status epilepticus. I am not sure that the case of Gage can bear the weight placed upon it as an exemplar of personality and psychological change resulting from focal damage to this area of the brain. There is plenty of subsequent evidence, but it is amazing how just a few facts can fuel an entire narrative which adds up to little more than a popular myth with a very shaky scientific foundation.

It took a Canadian-American neurosurgeon called Wilder Penfield [1891-1976] to take the mapping of brain function to a new level of sophistication. His innovative approach to treating patients with epilepsy led to the use of brain stimulation with electrodes in patients having their neurosurgical procedures under local anaesthesia, in order to minimise the collateral damage from the ablative techniques being used. In the course of this work he was able to localise the exact position on the cerebral cortex responsible for various motor and sensory functions. This led to the graphic representation of the parts of the body on, for example, the motor cortex to illustrate where the neurons responsible for a particular anatomical structure were found. The cortical homunculus illustrated the parts of the body to a scale representing the respective proportion of nerve cells responsible for that area. Since then a great deal of detail has been acquired linking specific areas within the brain to particular regions or functions.

There is a deeper problem, however, and it concerns the source of conscious awareness. Philosophers and theorists have struggled with this for hundreds of years. How might we explain the means by which even our advanced understanding of neurophysiology

The Thinker by Auguste Rodin.

and biochemistry can somehow produce the uniquely personal experience of self-awareness? The movie in my head seems to generate more than just sensation but is also responsible for emotion, ideas, intellect, memory, mental imagery, and will. It is as though we have a set of mental capabilities. Consider what happens when we awake from the state of insensibility produced by a general anaesthetic. As the anaesthetic agent is metabolised and wears off we begin to regain our motor and sensory capacity. The senses may be fuzzy and indistinct at first and the motor control will likely be uncoordinated, but we steadily regain precise function. At the same time the movie in our mind begins to run again. It may be unclear at first, but soon the feeling of what it is like to be in this state returns and the subjective experience of being awake and being able to take in and appreciate our surroundings gets back to normal. It is this fully-fledged phenomenal character of what it is like to be me, my hopes and fears, my beliefs and desires; it is all of this that so eludes a clear explanation.

Neuroscientists and philosophers have struggled to try to explain and anchor conscious experience, by reducing it to neuronal activity and therefore to ion fluxes and basic physiological and biochemical processes. Some aspects of our inner experience, such as moral values and aesthetic appreciation, seem to be beyond reduction. The philosopher David Chalmers has provided some helpful clarity in discussing this issue. He considers that there is an 'easy problem' of consciousness and a 'hard problem.' To appreciate the contrast it might be helpful to think of the difference between brain states as distinct from mental states.

The easy problem can be illustrated by defining how sensory organs connect, how we learn and how memories are stored. Pulling away from a painful stimulus or detecting your name being called within the chaos of a noisy airport lounge – we have a basic understanding of how to go about addressing these 'easy problems.' We have worked out where the senses are generated, and which neuroanatomical pathways the nerve impulses follow, to get to the brain.

The hard problem is altogether more perplexing. Why is it that the phenomenon of living should feel *like* anything from the inside? There is a sense of 'aboutness' in our thinking – what drives that? Where do the mental states come from? It is the origin of this odd but extremely personal and real sense of our inner experience that constitutes the 'hard problem.'

From a philosophical perspective there are two polar opposite views to explain our neurological and mental lives. Although no one can claim to understand how it might work there are those who are wedded to the view that our consciousness just emerged from basic neurological activity. This amounts to the claim that while the constituent parts of the system cannot account for the resulting features of consciousness, it nevertheless somehow happens, maybe the result of some kind of mathematical pattern but, essentially, it is just a state of matter. It is an assertion, devoid of a mechanism. While there are various subtleties inherent in the world of philosophy, this might be categorised as property physicalism or the claim that basic physical processes can explain all higher order mental properties.

There are some neuroscientists who would be comfortable with a naturalistic or physical explanation and who refer to the phenomenon of consciousness as an illusion. It can be thought of as the notion that our brains essentially trick us into conjuring up an impression that the world is the way we experience it. The logical problem with this is that the argument is circular because one would need to be conscious in order to experience the illusion in the first place.

On the other hand, there are those who do not accept this naturalistic explanation and recognise an immaterial quality about certain aspects of mental activity. The implication here is that the mind is not wholly explained by the brain. We can easily distinguish the fundamental differences between brain states arising from the way our senses present us with data from the physical world. We can see the sun setting on the horizon, or we recognise the face of a friend in the crowd, or we note the tactile sensation of the wedding ring on a finger. Each of these examples has an obvious connection between sense organs and specific matter in the external world. How can we take the next experiential step and understand what it is like to enjoy the beauty of that sunset, or appreciate the abstract emotional connection with a friend, as we bring to mind the last interaction we enjoyed in each other's company? How about the love for a spouse that is symbolised by the wedding ring, not to mention any ambitions, ideas or experiences we may have shared? None of these more abstract mind states are linked with the material world in the same way as sensations are connected. The mind states involving ideas, emotion, intentionality, value, intellect and will form part of the 'hard problem.' To date there is no clear route to understanding how to solve it.

An attempt to simplify mind states to electrochemical activity destroys any semblance of a claim to rationality or meaning. Electrical synaptic activity, as it chatters away, may amount to fascinating neurochemical interaction but to claim that it may be considered to represent rational discourse, or emotional experience, is surely absurd. Neurological events, reduced to basic chemistry, bear none of the hallmarks of value or rationality; they merely result in action potentials racing around neural networks; they are not right or wrong, there is no connected value, meaning or logical force, they just happen. It is little wonder that the hard problem is so named. If only we could identify a neurological understanding of ethics, aesthetics, emotion, rational thought and the range of conscious experience that distinctively characterise the human mind. As we have seen in every other area, trying to explain the cause of a complex system by a reductionist approach fails to come close to providing a satisfactory set of answers.

Philosophers for centuries have struggled to understand the material and apparently immaterial components. This is why the so-called dualistic view (brain and mind are not identical), like that advanced by Descartes in the 17th century, has been helpful. It is clear that mental reality is intimately linked to and partly dependent on the brain but the brain, while necessary for consciousness, is not sufficient to explain it.

The Cambridge academic, C S Lewis [1898-1963], was both perceptive and rhetorically gifted in his analysis of this question. He presented an essay to the Oxford Socratic Club in 1944 in which he wrote: 'If minds are wholly dependent on brains, and brains on biochemistry, and biochemistry (in the long run) in the meaningless flux of the atoms, I cannot understand how the thought of this mind should have any more significance than the sound of the wind in the trees.' Lewis, of course, was a well-known Christian apologist. However, the views he expressed had been similarly articulated by J B S Haldane [1892-1964] who did not share his theism. Haldane made a name for himself in the fields of physiology, genetics, evolutionary biology, and mathematics. He wrote, 'It seems to me immensely unlikely that mind is a mere by-product of matter. For if my mental processes are determined wholly by the motions of atoms in my brain, I have no reason to suppose that my beliefs are true. They may be sound chemically, but that does not make them sound logically.'[41]

One of the most famous physicists of the 20th century, Erwin Schrodinger [1887-1961], considered that it was not possible that consciousness could evolve from unconscious matter and unconscious mechanisms. He expounded his thinking in the little book *Mind and Matter*[42] which is a record of the Cambridge Tarner lectures of October 1956.

The famous neurologist Sir John Eccles worked throughout his career to attempt to define the link between mind and brain. Eccles emphatically dismissed the materialistic theory of the brain, denying that it was merely a particularly sophisticated and complex computer. His view was a development of the dualism of René Descartes [1596-1650] accepting that there was an immaterial mind, which acts through the material brain. In addition to our physical world, there is a mental world, each reality impinging upon the other. In one of his lectures he used the illustration of the pianist (mind) and his or her piano (brain). He summarised his thinking in a book published in 1973, *The Understanding of the Brain*[43] and described himself as a 'trialist' (rather than a monist or dualist; although it is a form of dualism) in which the material and immaterial interact.

One of the intriguing and almost mesmerising developments in this area brings the weird and counter-intuitive world of quantum mechanics into the picture. The subject of quantum biology is beginning to take shape and it shares much of the weirdness of quantum mechanics. While it remains in the realm of the speculative, various workers are developing the idea that some of the unexplained aspects of the natural world may have a quantum explanation and consciousness is one of these. It remains fundamentally vague, but it has been suggested that in some way biologically 'orchestrated' coherent quantum processes occur within the cytoskeleton of neurons within the brain and that somehow our internal movie is the result. The proponents, Hammeroff and Penrose, have written a review but the concepts are wrapped in uncertain terms.[44]

So, pause and think about your conscious life for a moment. To imagine that there is a straightforward material solution to the questions we have raised is simply naïve. There are layers upon layers of enigmata in life, and they just seem to keep on coming. Let me ask an even more fundamental question, a question that gets us closer to the most fundamental issues of ultimate reality. This was the great question of Leibniz: "Why is there something rather than nothing?"

Take home message ...

Consciousness is a feature of life. It is fanciful to imagine that higher mental properties such as reasoning, computation, memory, and emotion just somehow emerged from irrational, inert building blocks. To do so takes a considerable measure of completely blind faith.

Cosmic consciousness? How grand is the design?

My own suspicion is that the universe is not only queerer than we suppose, but queerer than we can suppose.

J B S Haldane

WE HAVE ALL BECOME AWARE of various laws of nature. We learned about the work of great pioneers like Isaac Newton, Michael Faraday, James Clerk-Maxwell, and Albert Einstein [1879-1955], who between them helped to formulate and characterise the equations behind fundamental forces of physical interaction. These comprise the laws of gravitation, electromagnetic relationships and the important subatomic forces known as the strong and weak forces. Einstein is reputed to have observed that, 'The most incomprehensible thing about the universe is that it is comprehensible.' In fact the quotation is not quite accurate. He wrote an article in 1936 in which he stated, "The eternal mystery of the world is its comprehensibility … The fact that it is comprehensible is a miracle."[45]

Distilling the observations about reality into some general statements that hold true in all circumstances has been of great benefit in understanding the world and how everything works. Going beyond basic scientific observation, I would like to suggest that there is another fundamental law that holds true and is independent of

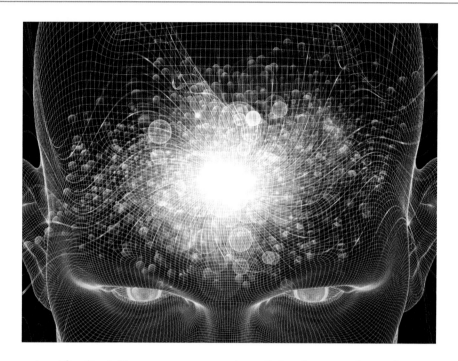

scientific discipline or preconception. It is, that *no physical entity can be the explanation of its own existence.* Nothing in the space-time universe is the explanation for itself. Some like to claim that it is possible to conjure a universe without any external agency. If true, that would certainly call this rule into question and suggest in some way that the universe may be able to explain itself. At first that sounds like an unhinged idea but it forms the basis for the writing of Hawking and Mlodinow in their book, *The Grand Design*[46] and so deserves more careful evaluation. Stephen Hawking [1942-2018] had one of the more remarkable intellects of our day and was rightly regarded as an outstanding mathematician, theoretical physicist, and cosmologist. The very questions that have been lurking in the background of our journey in this volume from the clinical sciences through physiology, biochemistry, and neuroscience towards the very basic chemical and physical principles, and building blocks of our world still remain and also underpin Hawking's approach. He asks the very same sorts of questions, right down to Medawar's questions of a child, how can we understand the world in which we find ourselves? How does the universe behave? What is the nature of reality? Where did all this come from? Did the universe need a Creator? Why do we exist? Why this particular set of laws and not some other and even the ultimate question of Leibniz, which materialism has stumbled at for centuries: Why is there something rather than nothing? When you look at that list, aware that Hawking's belief was that the scientific enterprise increasingly answers these very questions and can produce a better and more convincing account than philosophy or religion, one glaring issue rears its head. These are simply not the kind of questions that science is capable of answering. There is no boundary to the ability of science to answer the questions that it is capable of answering. However, it is logically beyond the boundary of science to adequately address such questions of origin. Amongst all the eight questions he poses in the *Grand Design*, only one of them is remotely accessible to a scientific answer. 'How does the universe behave?' is certainly a scientific question, all the rest are questions for philosophy. Hawking's contention is that philosophy has nothing to contribute; 'philosophy is dead' is the claim he makes. However, even that claim is not rooted in any scientific framework, so by his own explicit standards it is an incoherent assertion. It is, like the liar paradox we discussed in Chapter 6, self-referentially incoherent. His belief is that the universe can create itself out of nothing. You need just three ingredients – matter, energy, and space. So with stuff that has mass, with energy that permeates the universe, and with space which is ubiquitous, we are all set. Given that Einstein taught that mass and energy are essentially the same thing, we are down to two basic requirements. But, I hear you ask, how can you argue that the universe emerged from nothing when there is the requirement for basic materials with which to start? Surely this is illogical? 'Not so' would be Hawking's argument. His get out clause concerns the concept of negative energy. The secret behind the self-creation of the universe lies with negative energy. At the beginning of the universe a massive amount of positive energy came into being, as did, Hawking claims, an equal amount of negative energy. This ensures that the total adds up to zero! So, the story goes, there is no need for anything beyond the universe, it is capable of self-creation. Of course to sustain this story, he makes an appeal to the weird goings on at the atomic and subatomic level where, in the quantum world, conjuring something from nothing is commonplace. Recourse is made to quantum fluctuation, as if we can somehow reliably accept that therein is the adequate explanation.

You would be quite right to raise an eyebrow at this. For a start, a quantum fluctuation is not nothing. It is something. It is most assuredly not philosophical nothing – the absence of anything. To get his system going, Hawking needs, at the very least, a space so small, indeed an infinitesimally small and dense black hole. Most assuredly, even his theory, far-fetched as it may sound, still needs something to get it kick-started. So does Leibniz have his answer? I think not. How about his assertion that this 'spontaneous creation is the reason there is something rather than nothing, why the universe exists, why we exist. It is not necessary to invoke God to light the blue touch paper and set the universe going,' – does it stack up? Well it is certainly not spontaneous creation from nothing. Little wonder that John Lennox, the mathematician and philosopher of science has written: "Nonsense remains nonsense; even when talked by world famous scientists!"[47]

So, back to my as yet undefeated natural law that no physical entity can be an explanation for its own existence. It applies to every physical entity, including the universe itself. The only way to circumvent it is to abandon logic and, even with an appeal to the weirdness of the quantum world, it fails to get us where Hawking wants us to go. I always thought it interesting that some scientists will go to great lengths to defend a favoured idea. While we are all inclined to preferentially lock on to information that validates what we think, we can readily be drawn into accepting information and can be less critical than we ought to be if that information comports well with the position we are drawn to accept. What we really must do is to care whether the information we accept is, in reality, correct. There is even some work from clinical psychology (as we noted in Chapter 3) to suggest that the more educated a person is, the more cognitive contortions they will be prepared to perform to convince themselves that a particular case supports their worldview. The entire enterprise risks being ideologically driven, which is not an unbiased neutral position from which to start to address a particular question.

As for any physical entity, the underlying cause, by definition, needs to be external, beyond that entity. A cause for the physical universe transcends our understanding of reality. It cannot be part of the universe to be responsible for the creation of the universe because that is simply incoherent. The claim would have to be read like this: For the universe to create itself, it must, by definition, already be in existence. It does rather look like we need to posit a non-physical, immaterial, enormously powerful cause, beyond space and time.

Thomas Nagel has made some interesting and provocative contributions to the philosophical literature. One of his most controversial works is a little book about some of the very issues we have been exploring. *Mind and Cosmos* was published in 2012.[48] He sets out to demonstrate the cosmic significance of the mind body problem, the source of conscious experience with which we have been grappling in Chapter 17. Nagel is deeply concerned about the reductionist view that everything can be adequately explained by the physical sciences; he agrees that this is just not tenable. He is also concerned that the widely accepted view of how complex life came to be is also hard to believe. In fact, he suggests that it is reasonable to be sceptical of the two conventional views, first that life as we see it is, at source, the result of a sequence of physical accidents and, secondly, that in the evolutionary process that followed, again as a result of accident, a chain of genetic changes was enough for natural selection to yield the diversity of life we now recognise. He makes the case that his conclusion is not driven by any particular belief position (Nagel is an atheist), but that the available scientific evidence 'does not in this matter rationally require us to subordinate the incredulity of common sense.' If you were being unkind about this book, you might point out that Nagel encapsulated the preposterous nature of the apparent consensus of scientific opinion in a single sentence, whereas it has taken me more than 45,000 words to get to the same place!

So what does he postulate instead? In short, he entertains the notion that one ought to be open to the idea that the world is non-accidental. He appears to be sympathetic to the design argument but is perhaps less attracted to an idea of design that necessitates a designer. Most of us might find that a difficult concept to swallow. He does concede though that the failure of the orthodox reductive view leaves open the possibility of a genuine designer behind the universe. While this is not a position he is prepared to adopt, he appears to be seeking some kind of natural teleology rather than invoking agent causation.

However untenable the reductionist position seems to be, it is not short of some high-powered adherents. Take the Nobel Laureate, biologist Christian de Duve [1917-2013], a recognised expert on cell biology, who considered that 'Cells are so obviously programmed to develop according to certain lines ... that the word *design* almost unavoidably comes to mind ... [but] life is increasingly explained strictly *in terms of the laws of physics and chemistry*. Its origin must be accounted for in similar terms.'[49]

It will be evident that I, like Nagel, do not share De Duve's overly optimistic, reductionist views. We should remind ourselves of the view expressed by Paul Davies that there are only two options open to natural science in terms of explanation, natural law and chance. Are there any credible scientists convinced of the latter position? Without resorting to any kind of statistical argument, we have already seen how utterly improbable is the origin of life, or of information, or molecular machinery, or of all the amazing diversity, complexity, and fine-tuning we find in the natural world.

I find it quite incredible that anyone would be willing to back this position, but no less a person than the UK Astronomer Royal has expressed the view that the best explanation is 'a fluke.' Hedging his bets he said: "We know too little about how life began on Earth to lay confident odds. It may have involved a fluke so rare that it happened only once in the entire galaxy. On the other hand, it may have been almost inevitable, given the right environment." [50]

All of this may well create a sense of uneasiness, but I hope you can appreciate that I have attempted to build a case for putting the design hypothesis back on the agenda as a legitimate and evidence-based answer to some of these numerous, and as yet unexplained, questions. I sense that the problem is that the conclusion of genuine design carries the implications of postulating a designer, and while it may be the best explanation of the scientific data, it is ruled out of court because we can't find a way to fit it into our naturalistic methodology. According to Ernst Mayr [1904-2005], the evolutionary biologist and polymath J B S Haldane recognised the dilemma with the entertaining idea that "Teleology is like a mistress to a biologist: he cannot live without her but he's unwilling to be seen with her in public." [51]

It just seems too transcendental to be comfortable. Nevertheless it might be correct.

Take home message ...

So what about the remaining puzzle of ultimate reality? A universe capable of self creation? Clearly not! One must not deny logic just to avoid a transcendent conclusion.

The Golfer's Questions

A LOT OF GROUND CAN BE covered on the golf course, both literally and metaphorically. Golfers are obsessed with distance. They primarily want to know how far they will need to hit the ball, and that will be the major factor in determining their club selection. They

factor in the lie of the land, wind, spin, obstacles, and temperature, together with their strength and coordination, in an attempt to fashion the desired end result. Distance is a major issue. Sometimes you'll hear the quip that the most important distance is not how far you can hit the ball but rather that distance between your ears and what is going on in that space! If your attitude is not right, if you are tense, distracted and not concentrating or if your confidence is shaky, there is little doubt that your performance and your score will suffer. Quite what triggered the reflection that day I am not certain, but as four of us made our way down the sixth fairway of my local course one of my companions opined: "There are two things that no one knows how to answer. Where have we come from? And what are we here for?" Big time metaphysics certainly interfered with our concentration during that match! These are the very questions that have exercised thinkers and caused philosophical insomnia from time immemorial.

Scientific explanations may be appealing. Unfortunately, as we have seen, they appear to be totally inadequate, indeed natural science may not even, by definition, be able to get close to an explanation. Is it reasonable or even scientific to infer the existence of real design rather than simply the appearance of design? Well, we do it all the time. We know, without debate or hesitation when we see objects or arrangements of objects that are the product of a conscious and intelligent source. It is part of our every-day experience, so much so, that it becomes second nature to see the reality of design all around us. We would never hesitate to infer design when certain principles and characteristics are evident. Any preconceived and purposeful activity would automatically require genuine design. It is an ingrained feature of our physical environment and there is empirically detectable evidence that it also pervades the biosphere. So let's consider and characterise what the objective and rational base would be for the recognition of design. To be fair to the commonly accepted explanations in the natural sciences, we ought to establish whether natural laws or chance may satisfactorily answer the question of the origin of some complex physiological or biochemical system. If the answer is 'Yes' to either option, then we need go no further. If, on the other hand, the answer is 'No', then the additional possibility of deliberate contrivance or design needs to be considered. Take any of the examples we already examined in Section 2 of this book and it will quickly be clear that whether you examine the complement cascade, a molecular machine, the genetic code or the vital changes that take place in the circulatory system at birth; could any of these be produced by some deterministic repeatable natural law? Well, not by any law that has been identified so far.

Could they simply have occurred by chance? Not likely! In fact, so utterly improbable, any one of these examples represents an incredibly long shot. Clearly, neither of the commonly advanced explanations is satisfactory; in fact they are woefully inadequate. Some of you will have concluded that it is just ridiculously illogical even to entertain these options because they are so preposterous. What of design? It will be obvious that in principle all the features of design apply to each of these examples. While we have no clear idea of the mechanism that the design or manufacturing process followed, it is nevertheless clear in principle that a deliberate purpose-driven arrangement of each respective system is an obvious possibility.

By the time we reached the eighteenth fairway, we had not solved the conundrum or convincingly answered the questions. We had agreed, however, that the origin of biological life could not have been the result of some law-like process and, furthermore, no one was tempted to bet that the entire universe and life was a mere accident – by default, design is on the agenda. Even although some are, for a variety of reasons, repelled by the idea, it is evident that it remains a distinct possibility and all the golfers could clearly see the force of the logic.

Take home message ...

There is cold logic in the evidence for ultimate causation. Purpose driven contrivance carries the day!

Design all the way down?

WE CAN AGREE THE SCIENCE. We can accept the data. We sometimes differ, within the scientific and clinical community about the interpretation, whether it relates to figuring out how a particular chemical behaves in a reaction or what to make of the tangle of chaotic investigative information that may apply to a particular patient with a specific problem. It may be because of the way we reach decisions. In clinical surgery, it is often the case that active intervention has to be fast. Sometimes very fast, so in the heat of the moment the decision to operate or use a particular technique or even take a particular risk is a fast, intuitive, subconscious decision based on experience, context, and pattern recognition. It usually occurs with minimum effort and often when the whole picture is incomplete. In other circumstances, we may have the relative luxury of being able to pause and be more systematic and thoughtful, analysing and weighing the options by means of abstract reasoning and hypothetical thinking. Whether in the laboratory or the operating theatre the reality is that we overlay the data with a set of presuppositions concerning the kind of explanation we are willing to accept, and the action that we, therefore, adopt. When it comes to considering the possible role of design in nature, we will each naturally favour the option that fits our worldview. It is not so much an argument about a scientific question – like the 'turtles all the way down' tale in Chapter 4; it is more likely dependent on our philosophical starting point.

The materialist is constrained. Only physical reductionism will do. Anything else smacks of transcendence and is not only not scientific, but also just not acceptable. Remember Lewontin[33] and his anxious concern about allowing a divine foot in the door!

The design proponent at least has more territory to explore in a quest for a truthful understanding and can entertain the idea that something beyond the material realm may have played a role in the origin of life and its wondrous complexity.

In the surgical world, it is good practice to think proactively about the way to make decisions. It is of value, if at all possible, to slow down, anticipate the outcome more carefully and be aware of the confounding factors that can introduce bias. These can range from overconfidence or fatigue but equally can result from straightforward flawed decision-making.[52] In surgery, it would be no exaggeration to say that the outcomes can be life changing or life limiting, so the process is important. In the intellectual world we have been exploring here, it is also important to arrive at the best conclusion, to make the most accurate and reasonable interpretation of the scientific facts we can observe and to be careful not to poison our conclusion by some unjustified or value laden presupposition.

I had the opportunity to discuss some of the material I have included here in the Finlayson Lecture at the Royal College of Physicians and Surgeons of Glasgow in 2018. Many who attended on that occasion or who watched the recording online[53] provided the impetus to write this book. It occurs to me that the answers we find to these deep and mysterious difficulties are governed less by the scientific data and more by the philosophical suppositions we apply. At base it comes down not to a scientific conflict but to a worldview conflict.

I would suggest that there are basically a couple of frameworks that can be used to address the questions that I have raised in this book. What I have tried to set out has been a series of unexplained and maybe currently inexplicable difficulties. What are we to make of some of the mysteries that remain in clinical science? What is the origin of complex biochemical and physiological systems? How can we explain some of the exquisite elements of embryological development and the changes that take place at birth? Can we figure out a plausible basis for molecular machinery? What about information – where did the codes come from? We already noted in Chapter 14, and indeed we should not be surprised about, the perplexing question that bothered Charles Darwin. He realised the magnitude of the problem to try to understand the origin of first life. Even now we are not even close to finding an answer to that. Nor, as we have seen, are we making much of an inroad into the deep question concerning the means by which brain configuration and chemistry can manufacture subjective conscious experience.

It gets us down and in amongst the very basic questions of ultimate reality. Why is there even a universe at all, never mind the high degree of fine-tuning which characterises the laws and constants governing physical reality? All these examples bear the hallmarks of design and we have to brutally contradict our intuition to convince ourselves that the design is somehow illusory. Neither a theistic philosophy nor a purely materialistic approach can provide satisfactory explanations regarding the mechanism by which these various phenomena came to be. Logically, however, we have a huge problem to posit an explanation that screams 'Design' without a designing agent.

To contrast the two most basic worldview positions then reveals just how opposite they are in an approach to understand reality. For the materialist, ultimate reality comprises matter and energy. The theoretical physics community may wish to qualify that and discuss quantum field theories and try to suggest there may be a way to generate a universe from nothing. It is very clear, however, that their 'nothing' consists of something, namely a quantum vacuum fluctuation. As to where that may come from – they literally have no idea. So the materialist position is random, unguided, driven by (unexplained) natural law and essentially can be regarded as 'bottom up'. Any notion of a god would simply be a notion that is somehow secondary and is culturally driven by complex human society. For anyone with an honest enquiring scientific approach, the whole superstructure remains deeply unsatisfactory and features assumption and assertion at every turn.

For the theist, at least the design can lean on a designing agent and conceptually point to a creator and designer of the universe. God would be the ultimate reality in this view and matter and energy are contingent. It is a 'top down' scenario.

However uneasy one may feel about a theistic worldview, it is possible to avoid it. However, to do so, there is a host of unsolved questions that remain. Somehow the materialist needs to be comfortable with a framework where nothing produces everything, non-life produces life, randomness produces fine-tuning, chaos produces information, unconsciousness produces consciousness, and incoherent neural activity produces reason. To my mind the naturalistic, chance and necessity, starting point, doesn't get us very far. There is neither explanatory power nor mechanism. The theist may not have a detailed mechanism, but at least he or she has a coherent explanation in the form of agency. It is hard to kick against the teleology when so much of the evidence points in that direction.

Carl Sagan [1934-1996] in Episode 12 of *Encyclopedia Galactica*, when discussing the topic of surprising claims (concerning extra terrestrial life) pointed out "What counts is not what sounds plausible, not what we would like to believe, not what one or two witnesses claim, but only what is supported by hard evidence rigorously and sceptically examined. Extraordinary claims require extraordinary evidence."[54]

It seems to me, that any attempt to deny the implications of plain observation and reason comes with the considerable intellectual cost of trying to invent answers to the unsolved questions I have just outlined. It is clear that the appearance of design is an agreed, clear, and common sense conclusion from the scientific data; the burden of proof naturally rests with anyone wishing to pick a fight with that view. A teleological view comports with our natural cognitive perception; it is obvious. It is the implication that causes the visceral antagonism. Design necessitates a designer.

Richard Dawkins [1941-] protests in his book, *The God Delusion*,[55] that that is no answer. For him there is a follow-on question. Who designed the designer? The answer to that would inevitably lead us to the same issue again and again so we'd be into an infinite regress. However, if the designer is a being that is self-existent, that is, a being that necessarily exists by virtue of its own nature, then the enquiry about the design of the designer becomes meaningless. It seems to me that the logic displayed by Dawkins might be captured in a series of syllogisms, and, when it is laid out this way, it is easy to see the fatal flaw. He appears to argue as follows:

- Living things are complex, appear to display characteristics of design, and so it is highly improbable that they could have resulted from chance.
- If life were created, the creator, being at least as complex as the creation (if not more so), would be just as unlikely to have come into existence by chance.
- Therefore, God very probably does not exist.

The problem is that you only have to examine the flow of this argument for a moment to recognise that the conclusion does not follow from the premises. At best, all one could possibly conclude is that God, very probably, did not come about by chance.

In his contingency argument, Leibniz made the interesting distinction between entities that exist by means of dependence upon something else and those that don't. The former are contingent, the latter are considered 'necessary' entities by dint of their own characteristics. So, contingent reality would include everything that has a beginning. Everything that started to exist requires an explanation beyond itself. Virtually everything in the observable universe would come into this category. Contingent objects are not 'necessary' in the sense that they don't have to exist but rather, something has caused them to come into being. It is perfectly logical to conclude that contingent beings might not have existed at all, and this would be true of every day objects, of living things, and even of the entire universe. It provokes the question as to why the universe and all its contingent contents even exist at all.

Necessary entities, on the other hand, might include the curious concept of abstract objects. So, one can think of entities that might just be, and, because of their own nature, it is impossible for them not to exist. Some would argue that numbers and mathematical sets would be included in a category of necessary entities. For example, there is no cause for the number nine to exist, neither is there a need for an explanation for a set that includes all the positive integers. Theists would contend, of course, that God, a necessary being, did not come about at all, but has always existed. What we have is the suggestion that an external, non-contingent, non-material, ingenious, powerful being may be the explanation behind the design of life. I would support the logical idea that the only reasonable explanation for a contingent universe is that it exists because of the action of a non-contingent being. Such a necessary being would, by definition, be unable not to exist. The conclusion for contingent reality, the cosmos, physical law, matter, energy, life, and conscious experience is that all of this reality exists because of an unimaginably powerful, non-contingent entity, which is not part of physical reality but is immaterial, unconstrained by time and space, intentional and uncaused. It is little wonder that Leibniz formulated his version of the cosmological (contingency) argument[56] to demonstrate the existence of such a being. This fits the description that any theist would instantly recognise.[57]

The only way around this conclusion would be to show that the universe itself is a necessary entity. However, to sustain that view, the universe would have to be beginning-less, it would have to be past eternal. This approach has been torpedoed for both scientific and philosophical reasons. First of all, the standard teaching of modern cosmology indicates that the universe had a beginning. In his *Beginning of the Universe* paper presented in 2015 Alexander Vilenkin [1949-] made the point that 'The answer to the question, "Did the universe have a beginning?" is, "It probably did."'[58]

Together with cosmologists Arvind Borde and Alan Guth, Vilenkin was credited with the proof that the universe has been expanding throughout its history and so cannot have an infinite past. It requires a space-time boundary condition.

Even without any resort to current theories in cosmology, it is possible to argue that the universe must have a finite past. Since it is not possible to defend the possibility of an actual infinite number of things, this makes the idea of a past eternal state illogical. One can never reach an actual infinite number of anything, like intervals of time for example, because there would always be the possibility of successive addition of more seconds, hours or days. So, since arriving at the present time in a past eternal universe would involve reaching an actual infinite number and because transgressing an actual infinite is not possible, it follows that the universe cannot have a past without a boundary point – a beginning.

What can we make of all of this? Well, it is clear that scientific evidence and logical reasoning provide a very persuasive case for a designing agent behind all of reality. It is also clear that to try to swim against the tide of evidence and reason and claim that there is a material or natural explanation for everything that we see and experience is a claim that requires extraordinary justification. The question in my mind is this, 'How can you defend a claim that holds to a bottom up, 'everything just happened' type of argument when intuition, data and reason all powerfully indicate a designing agency;

a top down scenario?' The probability that the theistic position is correct is far higher than the unsupported materialistic viewpoint.

However uneasy one may feel about a theistic world-view, the appearance of design is inconsistent with the denial of a designing agency. If you wish to avoid the inevitable theistic claim, you need to be willing to accept that everything came from nothing and for no reason, that life arose spontaneously from inanimate stuff, and that the incredible fine tuning of the laws and constants of the universe just happened by some kind of sheer random chance. More than that, you need to buy in to the following: that the code subtending life, the astonishing repository of genetic purpose-laden information, somehow emerged randomly from a chaotic chemical background; that our rich subjective conscious experience was generated somehow from the complexity of the brain or from some kind of counter-intuitive, undefined quantum process; and that the very reason and logic you have used to think through the issues presented here is the mysterious outcome of matter and energy which betrays no sign of rationality. There is a good descriptive word for that belief system. Preposterous!

The mystery now is, having seen that there is no currently understood naturalistic mechanism which allows the production of observable reality, how could a theist offer a mechanistic explanation? How did the powerful, immaterial, intentional being go about producing matter, energy, time, life, consciousness, and everything else? There is no known or available mechanism. Intentional and genuine design does remain the best explanation to fit the facts, even although no one can offer an explanation for the explanation. That, in reality, is a common enough scenario. We frequently infer a particular explanation for the facts we observe without expecting or requiring an explanation for the explanation. Finding a message written in understandable language in a book or on a beach allows us to reach the very obvious explanation that an intelligent source was responsible, without knowing anything about the identity of the source. We do not require all the fine detail about the personal agent responsible for a written intelligible message to accept, perfectly reasonably and confidently, that a mind with intent and motive was responsible for the communication. We can confidently recognise a designing agent without requiring all the details about that agent – we can infer enough to know that such an agent was involved, and we can go as far as the data will permit in establishing certain characteristics the agent must possess.

Turtles all the way down? Perhaps not, but design all the way down looks like a very good fit indeed! The implications are far reaching, but will need to be the focus of another project.

Take home message ...

The choice is evident. The puzzle is in the nature of a worldview. Answering the questions of causation from a naturalistic 'bottom-up' approach runs counter to observed evidence. The weight of evidence supporting real design brings the theistic view to centre stage.

Index

References

1. Semmelweis, Ignaz. *Etiology, Concept and Prophylaxis of Childbed Fever.* University of Wisconsin Press; 1983.

2. Glasgow Medico-Chirurgical Society. Transcript of the minutes from the Glasgow Medico-Chirurgical Society held at the Faculty of Physicians and Surgeons of Glasgow. 1868.

3. *Strange earthquake waves rippled around Earth, and nobody knows why* [Internet], [cited 2019 Mar 5]. Available from: https://www. nationalgeographic.com/science/2018/11/strange-earthquake-waves-rippled-around-world-earth-geology/

4. National Vital Statistics Reports, Volume 64, Number 2, 02/16/2016. 119.

5. Asher, Richard. *Munchausen's syndrome.* Lancet Lond Engl. 1951 Feb 10;1(6650):339–41.

6. Asher, Richard. *Munchausen Syndrome.* Br Med J. 1958 Dec 6; 2(5109)(1415).

7. Cornwell, John, Editor. *The Limitless Power of Science.* In: *Nature's Imagination - The Frontiers of Scientific Vision.* Oxford: Oxford University Press; 1995.

8. Russell, Bertrand. *The Scientific Outlook* [Internet]. George Allen And Unwin Limited.; 1954 [cited 2019 Mar 5]. Available from: http://archive.org/details/scientificoutloo030217mbp

9. Russell, Bertrand. *Religion and Science.* Oxford: Oxford University Press; 1935.

10. Medawar PB. *The limits of science.* Reprinted. Oxford: Oxford University Press; 1989.

11. *Münchhausen trilemma.* In: Wikipedia [Internet]. 2019 [cited 2019 Mar 11]. Available from: https://en.wikipedia.org/w/index.php?title=M%C3%BCnchhausen_trilemma&oldid=880824231

12. Fitzwater, Marlin. *Call the Briefing! A Memoir: Ten Years In The White House With Presidents Reagan and Bush.* United States of America: Xlibris Corporation; 2000.

13. Doe PJ. *Old Glasgow Murders: Saturday 17th January 1976 – Two children found brutally murdered in Govan* [Internet]. Old Glasgow Murders. 2015 [cited 2019 Mar 11]. Available from: http://oldglasgowmurders.blogspot.com/2015/01/saturday-17th-january-1976-two-children.html

14. Boswell J. *Boswell's Life of Johnson* Abridged and edited, with an introduction by Charles Grosvenor Osgood [Internet]. Osgood CG, editor. 2006 [cited 2019 Mar 11]. Available from: http://www.gutenberg.org/ebooks/1564?msg=welcome_stranger

15. *Neural Crest Development - Embryology* [Internet]. [cited 2019 Mar 11]. Available from: https://embryology.med.unsw.edu.au/embryology/index.php/Neural_Crest_Development

16. Blamey SL, Imrie CW, O'Neill J, Gilmour WH, Carter DC. *Prognostic factors in acute pancreatitis.* Gut. 1984;25(12):1340–6.

17. Bettac L, Denk S, Seufferlein T, Huber-Lang M. *Complement in Pancreatic Disease—Perpetrator or Savior?* Front Immunol. 2017 Jan 17;8:1–11.

18. Galloway D, Galloway J. *Controlled Chaos: Surgical Adventures in Chitokoloki Mission Hospital.* John Ritchie Ltd; 2020.

19. Dawkins, Richard. *The Blind Watchmaker.* W.W. Norton & Company, Inc; 1996.

20. Kiserud T, Eik-Nes SH, Blaas HG, Hellevik LR. *Foramen ovale: an ultrasonographic study of its relation to the inferior vena cava, ductus venosus and hepatic veins.* Ultrasound Obstet Gynecol 1992 Nov 1;2(6):389–96.

21. Barclay, AE, Barcroft, J, Barron DH, et al. *A radiographic demonstration of the circulation through the heart in the adult and in the foetus and the identification of the ductus arteriosus.* Br J Radiol. 1939;12:505–17.

22. Kilner, PJ, Yang, GZ, Wilkes AJ et al. *Asymmetric redirection of flow through the heart.* Nature. 2000;404:759–61.

23. Reba, I. *Applications of the Coanda effect.* Sci Am. 1966;21:84–92.

24. Darwin, Charles. *On the Origin of Species* [Internet]. 1st ed. London: John Murray; 1859 [cited 2019 Jun 3]. Available from: http://darwin-online.org.uk/converted/pdf/1859_Origin_F373.pdf

25. Wolf, G. Friedrich Miescher: *The man who discovered DNA*. Chem Herit. 2003;21(10–11):37–41.

26. Pray, Leslie A. *Discovery of DNA Double Helix: Watson and Crick* | Learn Science at Scitable [Internet]. [cited 2019 Mar 5]. Available from: https://www.nature.com/scitable/topicpage/discovery-of-dna-structure-and-function-watson-397

27. Avery, Oswald T, MacLeod, Colin M, McCarty, Maclyn. *Studies on the Chemical Nature of the Substance Inducing Transformation of Pneumococcal Types: Induction of Transformation by a Deoxyribonucleic Acid Fraction Isolated from Pneumococcus Type III*. J Exp Med. 1944;79(2):137–58.

28. Johnson DS, Bai L, Smith BY, Patel SS, Wang MD. *Single-Molecule Studies Reveal Dynamics of DNA Unwinding by the Ring-Shaped T7 Helicase*. Cell. 2007 Jun;129(7):1299–1309.

29. *3D Animations - Replication: Mechanism of Replication* (Advanced). DNA Learning Center [Internet]. [cited 2019 May 14]. Available from: https://www.dnalc.org/resources/3d/04-mechanism-of-replication-advanced.html

30. Shapiro, James A. *A 21st century view of evolution: genome system architecture, repetitive DNA, and natural genetic engineering*. Gene. 2005;345(1):91–100.

31. Tour, James. *An Open Letter to My Colleagues* – James Tour – Inference [Internet]. Inference: International Review of Science. [cited 2019 Mar 5]. Available from: https://inference-review.com/article/an-open-letter-to-my-colleagues

32. Tour, James. *Animadversions of a Synthetic Chemist* – James Tour – Inference [Internet]. Inference: International Review of Science. [cited 2019 Mar 5]. Available from: https://inference-review.com/article/animadversions-of-a-synthetic-chemist

33. Lewontin, Richard C. *Billions and Billions of Demons*. 1997 Jan 9 [cited 2019 Mar 5]; Available from: https://www.nybooks.com/articles/1997/01/09/billions-and-billions-of-demons/

34. Davies Paul. *The Demon in the Machine*. Penguin; 2019.

35. Davies, Paul. *The Fifth Miracle*. Allen Lane. The Penguin Press; 1998.

36. Taylor, Katherine. *A New Thermodynamics Theory of the Origin of Life* [Internet]. Quanta Magazine. [cited 2019 Mar 5]. Available from: https://www.quantamagazine.org/a-new-thermodynamics-theory-of-the-origin-of-life-20140122/

37. Vandam LD, Abbott JA. *Edward Gilbert Abbott: Enigmatic Figure of the Ether Demonstration*. N Engl J Med. 1984;311(15):991–4.

38. Teasdale, G and Jennett, B. *Assessment of coma and impaired consciousness. A practical scale*. Lancet Lond Engl. 1974;304(7872):81–4.

39. Herculano-Houzel S, Lent R. *Isotropic Fractionator: A Simple, Rapid Method for the Quantification of Total Cell and Neuron Numbers in the Brain*. J Neurosci. 2005;25(10):2518–21.

40. *Passage of an Iron Rod through the Head* | NEJM [Internet]. New England Journal of Medicine. [cited 2019 Mar 5]. Available from: https://www.nejm.org/doi/pdf/10.1056/NEJM184812130392001

41. Haldane J. B. S. *Possible Worlds And Other Essays* [Internet]. 1927 [cited 2019 Mar 5]. Available from: http://archive.org/details/in.ernet.dli.2015.470199

42. Schrodinger, Erwin. *What is Life?* With Mind and Matter and Autobiographical Sketches. Reprint edition. Cambridge ; New York: Cambridge University Press; 2012.

43. Eccles, John C. *The Understanding of the Brain*. McGraw- Hill; 1973.

44. Hameroff S, Penrose R. *Consciousness in the universe: a review of the 'Orch OR' theory*. Phys Life Rev. 2014;11(1):39–78.

45. Einstein, Albert. *Physics and reality* - ScienceDirect [Internet]. [cited 2019 Mar 5]. Available from: https://www.sciencedirect.com/science/article/pii/S0016003236910475

46. Hawking, Stephen, Mlodinov, Leonard. *The Grand Design*. London: Bantam Books; 2010.

47. Lennox, John C. *Gunning for God: why the new atheists are missing the target*. 1st ed. Oxford: Lion; 2011.

48. Nagel, Thomas. *Mind and Cosmos: Why the Materialist Neo-Darwinian Conception of Nature Is Almost Certainly False*. Oxford, New York: Oxford University Press; 2012.

49. De Duve, Christian. *Vital Dust* [Internet]. Basic Books; 2017 [cited 2019 Mar 5]. Available from: https://www.basicbooks.com/titles/christian-de-duve/vital-dust/9780465090457/

50. Rees M. *Are we alone in the universe? We'll know soon* | Martin Rees. The Guardian [Internet]. 2012 Sep 16 [cited 2019 Mar 5]. Available from: https://www.theguardian.com/commentisfree/2012/sep/16/alone-in-universe-life-fluke-earth

51. Mayr E. *Evolution and the Diversity of Life:* Selected Essays. Harvard University Press; 1997.

52. Croskerry, Pat. *The importance of cognitive errors in diagnosis and strategies to minimize them.* Acad Med J Assoc Am Med Coll. 2003;78(8):775–80.

53. Royal College of Physicians and Surgeons of Glasgow. *The Finlayson Lecture 2018 - Enigmata ad Infinitum* [Internet]. 2018 [cited 2019 Mar 6]. Available from: https://www.youtube.com/watch?v=ZXcdJTQ9QiQ

54. Sagan, Carl. *Cosmos* s01e12 Episode Script | SS [Internet]. Springfield. [cited 2019 Mar 6]. Available from: https://www.springfieldspringfield.co.uk/view_episode_scripts.php?tv-show=cosmos-carl-sagan&episode=s01e12

55. Dawkins, Richard. *The God Delusion.* London; 2006.

56. *Philosophy of Religion. The Argument from Contingency* [Internet]. [cited 2019 Mar 8]. Available from: http://www.philosophyofreligion.info/theistic-proofs/the-cosmological-argument/the-argument-from-contingency/

57. Pruss, Alexander. *Leibnizian Cosmological Arguments* [Internet]. [cited 2019 Mar 8]. Available from: http://alexanderpruss.com/papers/LCA.html

58. Vilenkin, Alexander. The Beginning of the Universe. Inference [Internet]. Inference: International Review of Science. 2015 [cited 2019 Mar 8]. Available from: https://inference-review.com/article/the-beginning-of-the-universe

Image Citations

Page	Citation
32	https://www.shutterstock.com/image-illustration/closeupseismograph-machine-needle-drawing-red-714451780
34	https://www.shutterstock.com/image-photo/computer-screenshowing-mri-ct-image-1197120001
39	https://commons.wikimedia.org/wiki/File:Bruckner_-_M%C3%BCnchhausen.jpg G. Bruckner / Public domain
45	https://www.shutterstock.com/image-photo/calm-morningdumbarton-castle-scotland-uk-1454601284
51	https://en.wikipedia.org/wiki/Nicolaus_Copernicus_Monument,_Warsaw#/media/File:Copernicus_by_Thorwaldsen_Warsaw_02.jpg PublicDomain
55	L. Prang & Co, P., L. Prang & Co, C. C. & Hamman, E. (1873) Andre Vesale. , 1873. [Boston: L. Prang & Co. Boston] [Photograph] Retrieved from the Library of Congress, https://www.loc.gov/item/2016649781/
62	Public domain. Author; Anefo https://commons.wikimedia.org/w/index.php?curid=75100590 Original image retouched, corrected and colourised by David J Galloway, 2021.
65	Licensed under the Creative Commons Attribution 4.0 International license. Digitised for Codebreakers, Makers of Modern Genetics . https://commons.wikimedia.org/wiki/File:Peter_Medawar_c1969.jpg Original image retouched, corrected and colourised by David J Galloway, 2021.
83	https://www.techsupportofmn.com/bill-gates-reveals-top-5-healthcare-technologies-for-2019/

152   https://www.istockphoto.com/photo/spiral-strands-of-dna-on-the-dark-background-gm485038074-71694953

159   https://www.istockphoto.com/photo/t-cell-receptors-cd4-molecules-glycolipids-the-t-cell-receptor-activates-the-immune-gm1001608446-270731583

164   https://www.shutterstock.com/image-photo/coloniespenicillium-mold-growing-on-agar-1112007065

169   https://www.istockphoto.com/photo/cell-abstract-concept-microorganisms-under-microscope-gm1074985196-287770180

176   David J Galloway, 2021

178   https://www.shutterstock.com/image-illustration/neuronalnetwork-electrical-activity-neuron-cells-1691666992

181   Van Horn JD, Irimia A, Torgerson CM, Chambers MC, Kikinis R, et al. - Van Horn JD, Irimia A, Torgerson CM, Chambers MC, Kikinis R, et al. (2012) Mapping Connectivity Damage in the Case of Phineas Gage. PLoS ONE 7(5): e37454. doi:10.1371/journal.pone.0037454

183   Licensed under the Creative Commons Attribution-Share Alike 2.0 Generic license. Author; Douglas O'Brien https://commons.wikimedia.org/wiki/File:Le_Penseur_in_the_Jardin_du_Mus%C3%A9e_Rodin,_Paris_14_June_2015.jpg. Original image adapted by David J Galloway, 2021

190   https://www.shutterstock.com/image-illustration/frame-mindseries-backdrop-composed-human-278524988

197   https://www.shutterstock.com/image-photo/close-golf-ball-ontee-85163740

209   Created by NASA. Public Domain https://commons.wikimedia.org/wiki/File:Nasa_earth.jpg

About the book

Overall purpose and content summary

My purpose in writing this book was to provide a clinician's perspective on the evidence for real design in living things. It is written at a popular level. There are some technical details but these will be accessible to anyone with a basic understanding of human biology and those with a background in healthcare will immediately connect with many of the examples. Some are taken from real cases in clinical medicine and surgery as well as from the amazing connected systems that exist in immunology, endocrinology, physiology, biochemistry and neuroscience. Some specific design scenarios are also examined – one of the most spectacular being the astonishing changes that take place in the human circulatory system when the placental oxygen delivery is switched off and the lungs suddenly have to come into operation at the time of birth.

This book provides a powerful challenge to the naturalistic or materialistic view that the universe and life results from unguided 'natural' processes. The evidence accumulates to show just how untenable such a view really is. The case for real, rather than illusory, design is powerful and persuasive. It is time to consign outdated thinking and theories to the scrap heap rather than trying to resuscitate ideas that fly in the face of the evidence.

About the Author

Professor David Galloway MB ChB MD DSc is a surgeon based in the West of Scotland. An alumnus of the University of Glasgow, he graduated in medicine in 1977. His clinical training involved working in hospitals in Glasgow, London and New York City. His postgraduate academic work was focused on cancer research and in particular investigated aspects of cell division and the way in which it can be influenced by various environmental and dietary factors. He developed an academic surgical practice in Glasgow focusing on surgical oncology and metabolic surgery. Since 2014 he has provided intermittent surgical support to Chitokoloki, a Christian Mission Hospital in rural Zambia, and now holds registration with the Health Professions Council of Zambia. In 2015 he was elected to the role of President of the Royal College of Physicians and Surgeons of Glasgow, a post he held until December 2018. He has authored numerous clinical and scientific papers and is a Fellow of various international medical and surgical Colleges including the Royal College of Physicians and Surgeons of Glasgow, the Royal College of Surgeons of Edinburgh, the American College of Surgeons, the American College of Physicians, the Royal College of Physicians of Ireland, the Academy of Medicine of Malaysia, the Association of Surgeons of India, the Indian College of Physicians and the College of Surgeons of Sri Lanka.

He is married to Christine and they have two daughters and three grandchildren. He is a keen golfer and an avid reader of popular science, philosophy of science and religion, and current affairs. He is also in demand as a speaker on aspects of Christianity and apologetics.

Other books by the same author

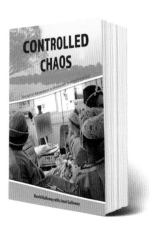

**Controlled Chaos. Surgical Adventures
in Chitokoloki Mission Hospital,**
(with Dr Jenni Galloway).
ISBN-13 978 1 912522 88 0
John Ritchie Publishing, 2020

**Follow the Science? But be wary where
it leads,**
(with Dr Alastair Noble).
ISBN-13 978 1 912522 98 9
John Ritchie Publishing, 2021